DISCOVERING THE BIBLE

JESUS
in
GALILEE

and other New Testament stories

RETOLD BY *Victoria Parker*

❖

CONSULTANT *Janet Dyson*

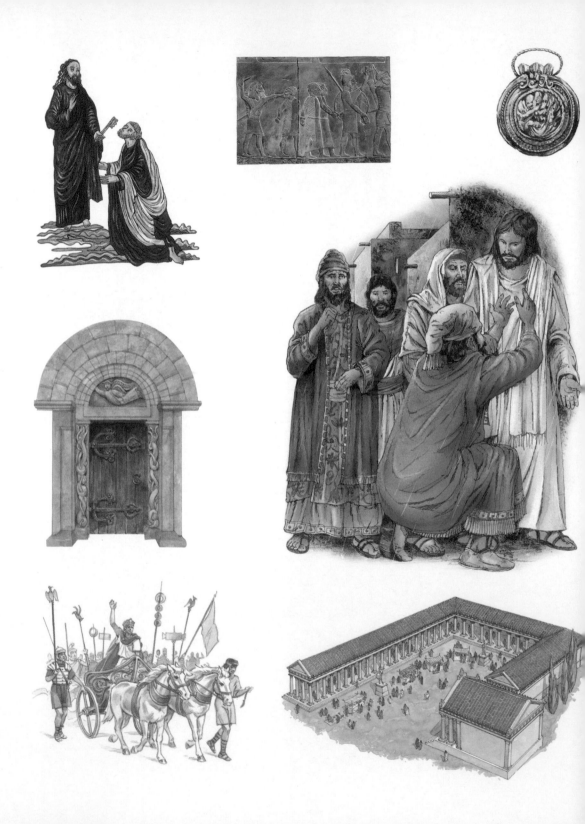

DISCOVERING THE BIBLE

JESUS
in
GALILEE
and other New Testament stories

RETOLD BY *Victoria Parker* ❖ CONSULTANT *Janet Dyson*

Published by Anness Publishing Ltd,
Blaby Road, Wigston, Leicestershire LE18 4SE

Email: info@anness.com

Web: www.annesspublishing.com

Anness Publishing has a new picture agency outlet for images for
publishing, promotions or advertising. Please visit our website
www.practicalpictures.com for more information.

Publisher: Joanna Lorenz
Managing Editor: Gilly Cameron Cooper
Senior Editor: Lisa Miles
Produced by Miles Kelly Publishing Limited
Publishing Director: Jim Miles
Editorial Director: Paula Borton
Art Director: Clare Sleven
Project Editor: Neil de Cort
Editorial Assistant: Simon Nevill
Designer: Phil Kay
Information Author: AD Publishing Services
Artwork Commissioning: Suzanne Grant and Lynne French
Picture Research: Lesley Cartlidge and Libbe Mella,
Kate Miles and Janice Bracken
Copy Editing: AD Publishing Services
Indexing: Janet De Saulles
Design Consultant and Cover Design: Sarah Ponder
Education Consultant: Janet Dyson

ETHICAL TRADING POLICY
Because of our ongoing ecological investment programme, you, as our
customer, can have the pleasure and reassurance of knowing that a tree is
being cultivated on your behalf to naturally replace the materials used to
make the book you are holding. For further information about this
scheme, go to www.annesspublishing.com/trees

PHOTOGRAPHIC CREDITS
Page 6, (BL), Sonia Halliday Photographs.
Page 20, (BC), The Stock Market.
Page 34, (BR), Frank Spooner Pictures.
Page 41 (BR), The Stock Market.
All other images from the Miles Kelly Archive

The Publishers would like to thank the following artists who have
contributed to this book:
L.R. Galante, Alessandro Menchi, Manuela Cappon, Francesco Spadoni
Studio Galante (Virgil Pomfret Agency: Sally Holmes, Rob Sheffield,
Vanessa Card, Terry Riley, Peter Sarson, Mark Bergin, Terry Gabbey (AFA),
John James (Temple Rogers)
Maps by Martin Sanders

Contents

Introduction

JESUS spent much of His time in Galilee, the northern part of the country where He had grown up. He worked his way way southwards, possibly visiting Jerusalem briefly several times. Here you can read about some of His teaching and miracles in Galilee, and then in Jericho and elsewhere.

Among the outstanding things He did were: feeding 5,000 people with just five loaves and two small fish; walking across the choppy waves of the sea; appearing to three of His disciples in His heavenly glory; and raising Lazarus from the dead.

Much of His teaching was in parables, simple stories based on everyday events which contained deep truths about God and His plans. Jesus used parables because it was easier for the people around Him to understand what He was saying in the form of a story. Some of Jesus' most famous stories are included here: the good Samaritan who cared for a stranger; the lost sheep that was found by a loving shepherd; the prodigal son who came home to say sorry; the proud Pharisee and the humble tax collector; and the unmerciful servant who didn't do to others what had been done to him.

Jesus's teaching remains as relevant today as it was 2,000 years ago. Among the subjects He covered were how to handle money and possessions, how to regard people we don't like, what God's plans are for life after death and how to get ready to meet God.

Jesus was a legend in His own time. People didn't know what to make of Him. Some thought He was just a great prophet, others thought He was one of the past

Jesus Christ
This painting of Jesus shows Him with a halo, a bright circle of light, around His head. Haloes like this first appeared in artwork in the 400s. The circle symbolizes perfection.

Judea and the Sea of Galilee
Jesus spent about three years travelling around Galilee teaching and healing the people that He found. He performed many miracles on and around the Sea of Galilee, such as walking on water, and feeding the 5,000 people.

prophets come back to life. He was watched with great interest because people in 1st-century Judea did believe that the promised Messiah, God's specially chosen servant, would come to them soon.

Jesus's followers were called disciples. Jesus had chosen twelve of these as His special companions, who are sometimes called apostles. One day, when Jesus was talking to His 12 disciples, He asked them who they thought He was. Peter, who acted as spokesman for the group, blurted out, "You are the Christ! The Son of the living God!" He got it right, although he hadn't worked it out for himself. Jesus said that it had been specially revealed to him by God.

However, even Peter and the others didn't really know exactly what that meant. The Messiah they expected was a military liberator who would chase the Romans out of Judea and set up a Jewish state which would be the envy of the world. The Romans had conquered all of Judea as part of their great empire, and they had left soldiers to keep the people of Judea in order. Some rich people made the best of the presence of the soldiers. Also, tax collectors were employed to collect money for the Romans, but this meant they were hated by the normal people. Most people resented the presence of the Romans, and wanted them out of their country. When Jesus arrived, saying He was the Messiah people expected Him to rid them of the Romans, but that was not Jesus's aim.

Jesus set about showing them, as well as explaining to them, who He really was. Soon after Peter's "confession" Jesus took Peter, with James and John, up a mountain where He was "transfigured" or transformed in front of their eyes. He glowed with heavenly glory. "That's the sort of Messiah I am," He was saying. "God's Son from heaven, not a soldier from earth."

When He fed the 5,000 with five loaves and two fish, He was demonstrating that as the Son of God He was also the Creator of all things and could provide what people needed. It was a lesson in both religion and faith. And when He walked on water, He was showing that nothing on earth was beyond His power to control.

His healing miracles showed that God cared for people in every part of their lives. With His raising of Lazarus from the dead He showed that death is not the end. Even this doesn't defeat God. There's something more to come.

Some people were so offended by the way Jesus wanted to change the old traditions and re-interpret the law of God that they dismissed Him as a trickster and a false teacher. Jesus was saying that important people had been misinterpreting the teachings of the Bible for generations. Although most people struggled to understand Him, no one who really watched Him or listened to Him with an open mind was ever quite the same again. And Christians today would say that hasn't changed down the centuries, either.

The woman from Samaria
The Samaritans had been hated by the Jews since the time of the Exile when the Samaritans had taken over the sacred city of Jerusalem. Jesus, though, preached to Samaritans as well, extending the word of God to everyone.

> **✥ JESUS IN GALILEE ✥**
>
> *Here you can read the stories of Jesus's teaching and miracles throughout Galilee, and in Jericho*
>
> FEEDING THE FIVE THOUSAND
> *Matthew, Ch. 14, Mark Ch. 6,*
> *Luke, Ch. 9, John, Ch. 6.*
> JESUS WALKS ON WATER
> *Matthew, Ch. 14, Mark, Ch. 6.*
> JESUS'S MINISTRY IN GALILEE
> *Matthew, Ch. 16 to 25,*
> *Mark, Ch. 9 & 10,*
> *Luke, Ch. 10 to 19.*
> OPPOSITION TO JESUS GROWS
> *John, Ch. 6 & 7.*
> LAZARUS RAISED FROM THE DEAD
> *John, Ch. 11.*
> JUDGEMENT DAY
> *Matthew, Ch. 25.*

Jesus and the Sea of Galilee

THE Sea of Galilee, and the region that surrounds it, are where Jesus spent much of His time, preaching to the people of the area, and teaching them about the new ways that He wants them to live their lives.

The Sea of Galilee is actually a lake, through which the River Jordan flows. This supply of fresh water means the Sea of Galilee is home to great numbers of fish, such as carp and tilapia, also known as Saint Peter's fish. The fishing grounds in the Sea of Galilee were famous throughout the Roman Empire, so the people of Galilee were able to export a lot of their catch, they would sell it to other countries. The Sea of Galilee is 211m below sea level and is surrounded by steep hills. This means that fierce storms can start on the lake at almost any time. Jesus and His disciples were sometimes caught out on the lake in these storms, but Jesus was miraculously able to calm the waves and get everyone safely to shore.

The fact that Jesus grew up in Galilee is reflected through all the Gospels. Many of His miracles and His parables relate to the type of work that ordinary people at this time would have done, and relate to the sorts of agriculture that would have been familiar to people at the time. Not only is Jesus drawing on the sort of experiences He would have had growing up, but He is telling His stories using characters and places with which His audience are familiar. When Jesus performed a miracle and fed 5,000 people with five loaves of bread and two fish, the fish that He used were almost certainly tilapia or carp, caught by local fishermen in the Sea of Galilee.

Throughout Jesus's parables we see a similar situation. He talks about agriculture, about farmers, and vineyards, and He uses the relationship that the Jews had at the time with people like the Samaritans to make His point. Ever since the time of the Exile, the Jews had hated the Samaritans, who were the people that the conquering Babylonians had moved to the sacred city of Jerusalem. Jesus uses this in His parable of the good Samaritan. He chose someone that His audience believe will not help the injured man to make the point that race and colour do not matter in God's kingdom, that the hated Samaritan who helped is more the man's neighbour than the priest and the Levite who did not.

Jesus's ministry in Galilee was a mission of preaching and healing. He healed a wide range of problems, paralysis, blindness, leprosy, demon possession. He even raised people from the dead. There were many people at the time who claimed to be able to cure people of these problems – Jesus was different not only in that He could genuinely cure them of their illnesses, but He did not use the sort of elaborate rituals that many people would have used to try to impress the audience. Jesus's power and authority over evil is unquestionable, so a single word of command was enough.

Jesus is also remarkable in that most of the miracles that He performed are not in order to show how powerful He is. He pities people for their suffering, and because He is the Messiah, the son of God, He is able to cure these people miraculously. When He is not healing people He is still helping them, such as when He feeds 5,000 people with five loaves and two fishes, or when He calms the storm, or even when He turns water into wine at the marriage in Cana. He is not reserved about what He is able to do, He helps miraculously because He is the Christ.

There are, though, exceptions to this. When Jesus walked across the water to reach His disciples, He was not helping anyone. But in this case He was teaching His disciples, He was making it clear to them who He was, and making it clear to Peter that faith can achieve anything.

We can see on this map the areas of some of Jesus's miracles, and some of people He healed and the events in His life.

Roman influence

The influence of Rome runs through the whole of the New Testament. Jesus was raised during the occupation, and was crucified according to Roman law. While there were problems with the Romans, as far as the people of Judea and Galilee were concerned, they gave a great deal to the people. Their buildings were very advanced for the time, for example, this is a magnificent Roman amphitheatre. By AD200 the Romans had built over 80,000km of good roads through their empire.

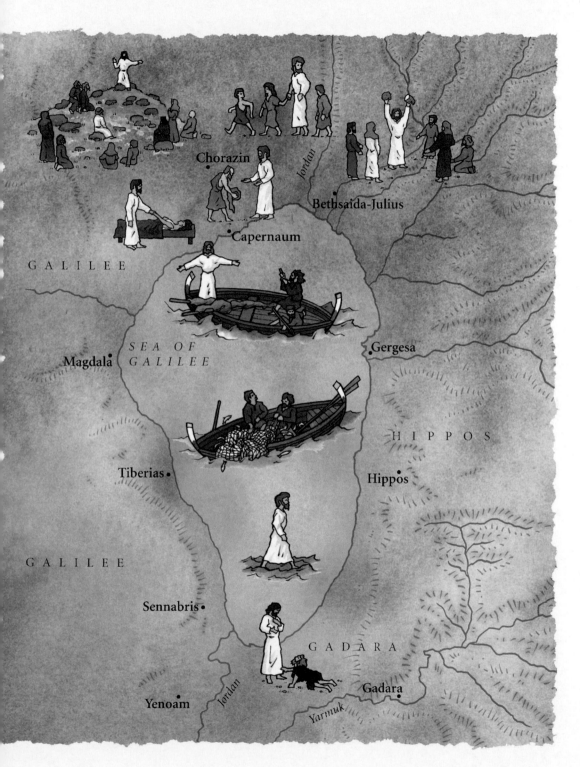

Chorazin

Jordan

Bethsaida-Julius

Capernaum

GALILEE

SEA OF
GALILEE

Magdala

Gergesa

H I P P O S

Tiberias

Hippos

GALILEE

Sennabris

GADARA

Yenoam

Jordan

Gadara

Yarmuk

Feeding the Five Thousand

THE twelve disciples had accompanied Jesus on His travels for many months. They had also spent several weeks in pairs on the road. Without Jesus present, they taught His message, healed lepers and cured diseases. By the time they rejoined their master, they were exhausted.

Times were even more trying for Jesus. The crowds grew bigger every day. However, many of the Pharisees and Sadducees refused to accept Jesus's teaching. They longed to get Him out of the way. Finally, on top of everything else, Jesus's cousin, John the Baptist, had been executed after spending several months in King Herod's dungeons.

One day Jesus and His 12 friends got into a little boat and sailed away from the crowds across the Sea of Galilee towards the quiet northern shore. They all urgently needed some rest and some peace and quiet.

At last it was peaceful! The sounds of the crowds were blown far away by the wind. Jesus and the disciples could hear nothing but the comforting swish of the sea, the gentle flap of the sail and the friendly cries of the seagulls.

However, the hundreds of people on the shore weren't going to be put off. On foot and on donkeys, they set off at once racing round the coast, joined by others they saw on the way. By the time Jesus's boat reached the far shore, to his surprise there was a massive throng waiting in anticipation for Him.

Instead of getting angry, Jesus just sighed.

"Look at them milling about," He said gently. "They're like sheep without a shepherd."

As the disciples guided the boat in the people started clamouring for Jesus to heal them. Even though Jesus was tired, He agreed to stay and the crowd settled down. Putting His exhaustion aside, Jesus began to speak. . .

Jesus was still preaching to the massive crowd when it began to grow dark.

"Master," said the disciples, "it's getting late now and we're a long way from anywhere. You should tell everyone to leave and find some food and a place to stay."

"You give them something to eat," Jesus replied bluntly.

The disciples looked at each other anxiously. They thought there must be over five thousand people listening to Jesus. How were they going to be able to feed them?

"We have only 200 denarii between us," they protested.

Washing rituals
The Pharisees had many religious ceremonies. This is one of the ritual baths they used for washing as a sign of spiritual purity. Jesus taught that people became pure by saying sorry to God and by living His way, not by taking part in ceremonies.

Popular catch
The carp fish, shown above, was one of the main fish living in the Sea of Galilee at this time, so it was a fish often caught by fishermen. It may well have been the sort of fish Jesus had in the story.

Loaves and fish
This ancient mosaic shows the kind of loaves and fish Jesus might have used. The picture reminded people that Jesus could provide for all their physical needs. It also reminded them that anything offered to Him, however small, could be used by Him to do good.

> *Taking the five loaves and the two fish he looked up to heaven, and blessed and broke the loaves.*

"Even if we find somewhere to buy bread, we would need a fortune to be able to buy enough food for everyone here. There won't be anywhere near enough to go around."

"All we've got at the moment is what this lad has brought with him," Andrew added, guiding a young boy with a basket through the crowd. "Five loaves of bread and two fish. But they're not going to go very far among this many people!"

"Tell everyone to sit down," Jesus said quietly, taking the basket from the boy. When everyone was settled, He said a blessing over the loaves and the fish and broke them into

pieces. "Now share them out among the people," He instructed His disciples calmly.

To everyone's utter astonishment, there was more than enough bread and fish to satisfy everyone. It soon became clear that there would be enough leftovers to fill 12 whole baskets.

Baking bread
In Bible times, fire was usually lit inside the stone oven rather than underneath it. When the stones were hot, the fire was raked out and dough placed on the sides (sometimes even on the outside) of the oven where it baked. The bread came out looking like flat rolls, or fat pancakes.

Fishing nets
The fish Jesus used were caught in the Sea of Galilee. Fishermen either dragged nets behind their boats or cast them from the shore.

❦ **ABOUT THE STORY** ❦

Jesus was the host at this gathering, and took the responsibility of feeding all of the people. His miracle reminds us that Jesus, the Son of God, is the Creator and Sustainer of all things and that we are dependent on God for all our needs. It also reminds people that Jesus not only cares for the physical needs but also our spiritual needs.

Jesus Walks on Water

THE news rippled through the crowd that Jesus had used only five loaves and two fish to feed them.

"A miracle! Jesus must be the prophet that was promised to us," came the delighted cries. "Let's make Him our king!"

The people began to shout for Jesus to speak again. So Jesus turned back to the disciples huddled round Him.

"They're obviously not going to let me go for a while," He said to his 12 friends, kindly. "Why don't you start back without me?"

"But Lord, how will you..?" the disciples protested.

"Don't worry, I'll catch up," Jesus reassured them.

Wearily, the friends went down to their boats, climbed aboard and sailed away from the crowds.

Eventually people went home. Jesus wanted to talk to His Father, so He climbed into the hills to pray.

Meanwhile, the disciples were in trouble. A strong wind had blown their boats off course, into the choppy open waters. The night grew darker. They lost sight of the shore and the stars. They felt lost and afraid. As they searched for the glimmer of the dawn, they saw a pale glow in the darkness that lengthened into the white form of a man.

"It's a ghost!" the disciples cried, shrinking away in fear.

Then a familiar voice called to them above the gusting wind and the crashing waves.

"Don't be afraid!" it said. "It's me, Jesus!"

The disciples didn't know what to think. So many strange things had happened to them recently! Nothing was as it seemed any more.

Fishing boat
Boats like this were used on the Sea of Galilee. They were powered by a single sail and by oars. They were large enough to carry about a dozen men.

Sea food
This plate from Roman times is decorated with images of sea foods. People using decorations like this shows how important the sea was to people in Biblical times. Not only was it used for food and water, but also transport and trade.

PETER LEARNED AN IMPORTANT LESSON: HE COULD DO WHAT JESUS WANTED WHEN HE HAD COMPLETE FAITH IN JESUS AND TRUSTED HIM ENTIRELY. PEOPLE NEED GOD'S HELP TO DO HIS WILL. ∾

Anchor
Just as an anchor stops a ship drifting, so God's promises to us are firm and secure. They will keep us safe from harm.

Peter peered forwards, squinting through the darkness. "Lord, is it really you?" he cried. "If it is, tell me to come to you across the water."

"Come! Come!" Jesus's voice floated across to them.

> ❝ *When they saw Him walking on the sea they thought it was a ghost.* ❞

Peter swallowed hard and stood up. Gingerly, he made his way to the edge of the rocking boat and looked down into the swirling water. Then he lifted his head and focussed on the white shape in the distance. "It is Jesus, my friend," he said to himself. "Jesus has told me to come to Him." Peter stepped out of the boat.

The other disciples couldn't believe it. Far from plunging into the depths, Peter was walking away from them on the water! Step by step across the tossing waves he went, as steadily as if he was strolling along the sand on the shore, not walking across the sea itself in a storm.

But when Peter looked down at the seething water beneath him, his courage suddenly deserted him. "Help me, Lord!" he yelled in a panic. "I'm sinking!"

Jesus reached out a hand and heaved Peter up. "You have such little faith in me! Why did you doubt me?"

Jesus put His arm around His friend and guided him back to the boat. Instantly, the waves and wind fell calm. The other disciples in the boat had seen it all.

"Lord!" they cried, falling at Jesus's feet. "We know you truly are the Son of God!"

Navigation

At this time people used the stars to guide them at night. This picture shows the Pole Star and Ursa Minor at the centre, with the constellations (going clockwise from the left) Draco, Cephius, Cassiopeia, and Camelopardus.

High places

Mountains and hills in Judea provided many places to go to, to pray alone. It is not likely that the Jews felt they were nearer to God in high places, but that mountains reminded them of God's power.

❖ **ABOUT THE STORY** ❖

This is one of Jesus's strangest miracles. Most of His miracles helped people by healing or feeding them. This one is meant to teach the disciples about Jesus. No one can walk on water, and only God could overrule the laws of nature. Hence Jesus was showing them, in a way they could not doubt, that He was God in human form.

Peter the Rock

ONE day Jesus and His disciples were on the road to Caesarea Philippi. For once, there was no one else around and they could talk freely. Jesus seized the opportunity to have a very important conversation.

"I sometimes call myself the 'Son of Man'," Jesus said, as they tramped along the dusty path. "What do people think I mean by that? Who do people think I am?"

The disciples shrugged.

"Some say you are John the Baptist..." one began.

"Or the great prophet Elijah come back to us..." interrupted another.

"Or one of the other prophets from the old days, like Jeremiah," suggested another.

Jesus shook His head and sighed.

"But who do you think I am?" He asked quietly.

Peter replied without a moment's hesitation. "You are the Christ, the Son of the living God!" he said.

Jesus smiled.

"You have been blessed, my friend," He told Peter. "My Father in heaven has helped you to understand this."

Jesus rested His hand on Peter's shoulder.

"You are Peter the rock," said Jesus, "the rock on which I will build my church – a church that nothing will be able to destroy, not even death. Peter, I will give you the keys to the kingdom of heaven, and whatever laws you lay down on earth will stand in heaven too." Jesus looked around at the little group.

❧ ABOUT THE STORY ❧

When Jesus called Peter "The Rock" he was playing on the meaning of Peter's name, which is "stone". The message he and the others preached was like a "rock", strong and firm. Peter also became the first leader of the church and the first disciple to preach to non-Jews. Peter was an effective foundation upon which the church could be built.

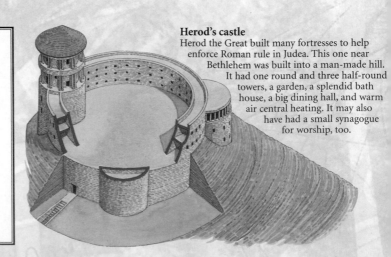

Herod's castle

Herod the Great built many fortresses to help enforce Roman rule in Judea. This one near Bethlehem was built into a man-made hill. It had one round and three half-round towers, a garden, a splendid bath house, a big dining hall, and warm air central heating. It may also have had a small synagogue for worship, too.

"It is most important that you tell no one that I am the Christ. No one at all. But since you all know who I am, I should tell you what is going to happen to me."

Jesus's tone was deadly serious. He breathed a deep sigh.

"The time is coming soon when I will have to go to Jerusalem, and things will become extremely difficult there. The elders and the chief priests and the scribes will make a great deal of trouble for me and I will have to go through a lot of suffering. Eventually, they will even put me to death." The disciples gasped. "But," Jesus said, holding up His hand to silence them before they could protest, "on the third day after my death I will be raised back to life again."

> **" And He began to teach them that the Son of Man must suffer many things. "**

Peter couldn't get over what Jesus had just said.

"God forbid, Lord!" he cried, absolutely horrified. "Such dreadful things should never happen to you!"

Jesus drew Himself up, straight and determined.

"To take an easier way would be to give in to the devil's temptations," he explained. "Peter, you are seeing things through human eyes. You aren't seeing them as God does."

Peter sadly hung his head.

"Now," Jesus announced to all the friends, His voice kind but firm. "Anyone who wants to follow me is going to have to sacrifice all their pleasures and comforts. They will have to be prepared to face danger and hardship, pain and suffering. To follow me even to the death, if needs be."

Jesus looked at the disciples' anxious faces.

"But I tell you this," He assured them. "Anyone whose main concern is to keep safe and content will lose the chance of eternal happiness. Yet anyone who gives up their life for the sake of me and my teachings will live for ever in heaven. For what good is it if you win the whole world, but lose your soul in getting it? And what could be more precious to someone than their soul? Believe this – the Son of Man will one day come again in heavenly glory, and everyone will then be repaid for all they have done."

As they walked on, the disciples' minds were perplexed and their hearts heavy with dread at what Jesus had warned lay ahead.

Jesus and His disciples
This carving depicts the moment when Jesus told the disciples that He would be killed and then raised in Jerusalem.

Peter and the keys
This painting shows Jesus giving Peter the keys of heaven. This shows that the disciples had the "key message" which enabled people to find God.

Herod's coins
The Romans allowed the Jews to mint their own coins. The coins here were minted by Herod the Great, Herod Agrippa or Herod Antipas. Usually Jewish coins had pictures of plants or man-made objects on them.

A Vision of Glory

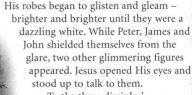

ABOUT a week after Jesus's solemn conversation with the disciples, He asked Peter and the brothers James and John to go with Him up a mountain to find a quiet place to pray. They left the other disciples at the foot of the slopes with a bustling crowd. The four friends reached a peaceful spot and settled down to pray.

Peter, James and John were so wrapped up in their prayers that they had no sense of time passing. It could have been minutes, it could have been hours.

As Jesus prayed, His face turned towards heaven. He was utterly motionless, like a living, breathing statue. It was as if He was present only in body and not in spirit; as if He couldn't hear the birds wheeling and crying overhead nor the wind gently ruffling His hair.

When the three disciples had finished praying they turned to watch Jesus, not daring to move or speak. They waited and waited... and still Jesus went on praying. After a while, Peter, James and John felt as if they were sinking into a trance themselves. Then something seemed to stir them. They shook themselves awake to an amazing sight.

Jesus's face began to shine with an inner glow. It grew lighter and lighter until it was more radiant than the sun.

His robes began to glisten and gleam – brighter and brighter until they were a dazzling white. While Peter, James and John shielded themselves from the glare, two other glimmering figures appeared. Jesus opened His eyes and stood up to talk to them.

To the three disciples' astonishment, they realized that the heavenly newcomers were Moses and Elijah – the mighty law-giver and the greatest of the prophets! They heard them discussing with Jesus the terrible trials He was to face in Jerusalem – what He was going to suffer and the way He was going to die. And as Peter, James and John watched and listened – totally transfixed – they saw the great prophets Moses and Elijah start to move away, gradually beginning to fade into the distance.

> " *His face shone like the sun, and His garments became white as light.* "

"Master!" Peter cried out urgently, not wanting the magnificent vision to end. "It's wonderful that we're here. Allow us to make three shrines – one for you, one for Moses and one for Elijah..."

Mount Tabor
This is one possible site of Jesus's transfiguration, where He appeared as a heavenly being to Peter, James and John. There was a town on its top even in Jesus's day, so it wouldn't be easy to be alone there. Some scholars think that the transfiguration happened on the more remote Mount Hermon.

PETER WANTED TO BUILD SHRINES BECAUSE HE WANTED TO KEEP THE FIGURES ON EARTH. HE HAD TO REALIZE THAT SPIRITUAL EXPERIENCES CANNOT BE PRESERVED.

As he was speaking, a cloud surged above them, blotting out the luminous skies and throwing darkness over the ground. A voice boomed down from heaven, saying, "This is my Son, my Chosen One; listen to Him!"

At the sound of the almighty voice, the three disciples fell on their faces in terror. When it had finished speaking, they felt the cloud's shadow lifting from over them. They felt Jesus's gentle touch upon them and heard His familiar voice saying, "Get up. Don't be afraid."

When Peter, James and John looked up, Jesus was alone – just a seemingly ordinary man, as before.

As the three stunned disciples followed their master down the mountain, Jesus told them not to tell anyone at all what they had seen and heard, not until He had risen from the dead.

Peter, James and John were bewildered. There were so many things that the three of them didn't understand.

"What do you mean, you will 'rise from the dead'?" they asked Jesus. "Besides, why should the Son of Man suffer and be condemned to death? And why does it say in the scriptures that Elijah must return before all this is to happen?"

"Elijah's return is to prepare the way for the Son of Man – and in fact he has already been here," Jesus explained. "But the people did not recognize him. They

did to him exactly what they liked, just as they will do to the Son of Man." At last the three apostles realized with a shiver that Jesus was speaking of John the Baptist.

Jesus with Moses and Elijah
Moses gave the Old Testament law to the Jews, and Elijah was the greatest prophet of the Old Testament. Jesus came to complete their work.

John the Baptist
John the Baptist was Jesus's cousin, who prepared the way for the coming of Jesus. He was executed when Herod promised his step-daughter anything she wished after she danced for him. Her mother told her to ask for John's head because he had criticized her marriage to Herod.

> ❖ **ABOUT THE STORY** ❖
>
> *Jesus had taught that He came from heaven, and this incident showed the disciples what heaven was like. It helped them to believe that He really was the Son of God, as Peter had declared a few days earlier. They saw the purity and holiness of heaven as a bright light. Visions of God's holiness often make people realize just how sinful they actually are.*

Moving Mountains

JESUS, Peter, James and John came down from the mountain to find a noisy crowd surrounding the disciples who had remained behind at the foot of the slopes. The companions hurried to find out what was going on. Suddenly Jesus was swamped by people all shouting at once.

Jesus raised His hands and motioned for everyone to be quiet. Then He spoke. "Will someone please tell me what you are squabbling about with my disciples?"

An anxious-looking man immediately stepped forward. "Teacher, I came with my son to find you. He's ill. It's like there's an evil spirit in him which suddenly throws him to the ground. He foams at the mouth and jerks horribly, then stiffens like a board. I asked your disciples to cast out the evil spirit from my son, but they couldn't."

Jesus looked around at the nine embarrassed and deeply puzzled disciples. Thanks to Jesus's gift of healing powers, they had been able to perform many miraculous cures on their own. But each disciple had tried to heal this particular boy, and no one had had any success.

"My faithless friends! How long must I put up with you?" Jesus scolded. "Now bring the child to me."

Jesus had barely laid eyes on the boy when he collapsed.

"How long has he been like this?" Jesus asked.

"From childhood," the boy's father sobbed. "It's very dangerous, too. It's like the evil spirit wants to kill him! My son has fallen onto the fire and even into water."

The child moaned and tossed.

"I beg of you," the upset man continued, "if it's possible to do anything, please help us."

> 66 *All things are possible to him who believes.* 99

"My friend," Jesus replied, "anything is possible if you only have faith."

F AITH IS NOT SOMETHING YOU CAN MEASURE IN THE SAME WAY AS WE CAN MEASURE LENGTH OR WEIGHT. FAITH IS SIMPLY TRUSTING GOD TO WORK IN HIS WAY. THE BOY'S FATHER ASKED JESUS TO HELP HIM TO PUT HIS TRUST IN GOD.

Mustard
Mustard seed is very small but the plant can grow as high as 5m (16 ft). Jesus was saying that faith doesn't need to be very big in order to have big results like "moving mountains". Mustard was an important seasoning in food in Jesus's time, so would have been familiar to the disciples.

Lunatics
The Romans believed that the moon affected people's minds. They called mentally ill people "lunatics" after the Latin word for moon, "luna". As the moon got bigger, so people got madder, they said. The Jews didn't believe this, and the boy in the story may have been suffering from some sort of epilepsy.

down and took the boy's hand in His own. At once, the child's fingers quivered. Then they tightened around Jesus's grasp. Finally, he opened his eyes, and Jesus helped the dazed child to stand up.

While the crowds were still with them, the disciples said nothing to Jesus about the healing. But as soon as they were on their own, they asked Jesus why He could cure the boy when they couldn't.

"It's because you have so little faith," Jesus explained. "Even if you had faith the size of a mustard seed, nothing would be impossible for you. You would be able to move mountains."

The father's eyes lit up with hope. "I believe you can help my unbelief!" he cried.

Jesus turned to the writhing body of the boy.

"Spirit! I command you to come out of him!" He ordered, sternly. "Never enter him again!"

Immediately, the boy began to thrash more violently than ever. Fits convulsed him, his arms flayed in the empty air and his legs juddered. The onlookers gasped as the boy gave a final groan and collapsed into a crumpled heap.

His father was left motionless with shock, appalled and terrified. But the crowd began to whisper.

"He looks as though he's dead," someone muttered.

Everyone fell silent as Jesus stepped closer. He bent

Charms
The Romans used lucky charms like this bulla to ward off evil spirits. The Jews did not believe that charms could defeat spirits. Jesus often cast evil spirits out of people to show that God was always more powerful than evil.

Fire
Fire was essential to life, but it was not easy to light so people kept them burning all the time. The boy could have fallen in at any time. This model is of an Egyptian fanning a charcoal fire to make it burn brighter.

❖ ABOUT THE STORY ❖
Perhaps one reason why the disciples couldn't cast out the evil spirit was that they had come to trust in the powers Jesus had given them, rather than in God himself. Jesus shows that there is no magic involved in healing or helping people. He wants His followers to trust God entirely, and not assume that because they've served God effectively once they can do so again by themselves.

Jesus and the Children

JESUS'S disciples had a lot to learn. While they were following Jesus down the road to Capernaum one day, they began a silly argument.

"Which one of us is the best, then?" was the question that started it all.

"Well," someone piped up, "I've known Jesus the longest..."

"Ah, but that doesn't necessarily make you the greatest," someone else quickly protested.

"I reckon it's him," came another voice, "because he's done the most miracles."

"No, no, no," another voice insisted. "I think it's whoever prays hardest..."

And so they went on... and on... and on. The disciples didn't think that they had been overheard. But when they had reached their destination and had settled into their lodgings, Jesus asked them, "So what were you discussing on the way down here?"

The 12 men fell into an embarrassed silence. None of the disciples could look Jesus in the eye. Some of them shifted awkwardly from foot to foot and began to fidget.

It was as if Jesus had heard every word. Or maybe He just knew what was in all of their hearts.

"If you want to be considered great before God," Jesus said, "you must put others first and yourself last. Here on earth, the greatest people are thought to be those who have the most servants to run around after them. But in the kingdom of heaven, the greatest people will be those who have willingly done the most to help others."

" *Let the children come to me, and do not hinder them.* **"**

Jesus reached out to a little child that was running by and she smiled as He drew her toward Him.

"Look at this simple, earnest child," He said. "Unless you give up your worldly values and become like this little girl,

---

❖ ABOUT THE STORY ❖

There was nothing sentimental about Jesus's attitude to children: He knew they could be as awkward as anyone else. He also knew they could teach people something about trust. He wanted to stop the disciples from discriminating against people. They did not think of children as fully human yet; Jesus accepted them, and everyone else, just as they were.

Capernaum
This was an important town on the north-west shore of the Sea of Galilee, close to where the River Jordan enters it. It was the home of Peter and other disciples, and was where Jesus began His ministry. He preached in the synagogue there shortly after He was baptised.

you will never even set foot in the kingdom of heaven. It is those who are selfless and giving like children who are the greatest in the kingdom of heaven. Their angels see God face to face. Always respect those who have a simple, childlike faith. For in doing so you'll be honouring me and my Father. If you sneer and look down on them, you'll end up wishing that you'd drowned yourself in the depths of the sea."

But the disciples didn't remember their lesson for long. Some weeks later, after Jesus had been preaching for the whole day, the disciples saw that some people were bringing their children to Jesus so He could bless them. While some of the little ones were shy and hung back, hiding behind their parents' legs, others ran round boisterously. The disciples began to shoo the children away, feeling sure that, at the end of such a long day, they must be annoying the weary preacher. But Jesus stopped them. "Don't send the children away. Let them come to me," He scolded, "for the kingdom of heaven belongs to them." Jesus bent down among them so the children could wrap their arms round His neck and climb onto His lap. "Unless you are like this – able to give yourselves wholeheartedly – you will never be able to enter the kingdom of heaven."

Children
Jesus used children as an example of faith and trust. Children do not usually have the same worries as adults, and took Jesus at His word.

God's provision
This is a receipt issued by a Roman tax collector. Jesus told people not to get worried about money and possessions, but to have the simple faith of a child and trust their heavenly Father to provide for their needs.

God's children
This picture shows that all people are God's "children". That is, He cares for them like a good parent.

The Rich Man's Question

JESUS stood up and drew His robes around Him, ready to take to the dusty road once more. But before He and His disciples were quite ready to set off, a man came running up to them.

"Wait!" he was crying. "I beg you to wait!"

The friends stood patiently while the man dashed up and knelt at Jesus's feet. The disciples were a little surprised, as the man was well-spoken and dressed in what were obviously very expensive clothes. It was strange to see such a wealthy person kneeling to anyone!

"Good teacher," the man panted, trying to catch his breath, "please tell me what I have to do to win eternal life."

"Why do you call me 'good'?" Jesus asked gently. "No one is good but God alone."

The man looked puzzled, so Jesus just answered his question with a kind smile.

"You know the commandments," He said, "Do not kill, do not pursue another man's wife, do not steal, do not lie, respect your father and mother, and love your neighbour as yourself."

"Master, I have tried my hardest to keep all these commandments ever since I was a little boy," the man said.

"Then there is only one other thing you must do," Jesus said, His voice low. "You must sell everything you possess and give every penny of all the money you make to the poor."

Dyeing clothes
Rich people in Biblical times, as today, liked to wear richly coloured clothes. Wool (and linen for rich people and priests) was dyed in vats like this.

The eye of the needle
Jesus's humorous saying about camels passing through the eye of a needle means that people who trust in their wealth or status cannot get into heaven. Only people who trust God – rich or poor – can enter His presence.

The man's eyes widened. Then his face fell, and he bowed his head. "Thank you, master," he said and slowly got to his feet and turned away.

> *Sell what you have, and give to the poor, and you will have treasure in heaven.*

The disciples watched the man trudge off down the road. He was deep in thought, his shoulders slumped and his heart heavy.

Jesus understood that He had just told the man to do a drastic, life-changing thing. He realised that it would be extremely difficult for him to carry out the instruction. Yet He also knew that it was a necessary for him to do to get to heaven. He sighed.

"How difficult it is for those who are wealthy to enter the kingdom of God!" Jesus remarked. "In fact, it is easier for a camel to pass through the eye of a needle than for a rich person to reach heaven."

The disciples were worried. After all, most people worked hard to be comfortably off. Very few people would find it possible to give away all that they owned.

"Surely no one will be saved then?" they asked Jesus.

"There are things that are impossible for people," He replied, "but with God, there is always a way."

As Peter listened and pondered, a thought struck him.

"Lord, we have left everything to follow you – our families, our homes, our possessions, our jobs," he said. "Is this enough?"

"Anyone who has done what you have done will receive a reward a hundred times better than what they have left behind," Jesus assured them, "and eternal life will be theirs."

The colour purple
The best and most expensive dye for clothes came from the murex, a shellfish in the Mediterranean. It gave a deep purple colour. Only rich people, like the man in the story, could afford it.

Flax
Flax grows in many parts of the world and has blue flowers. The stem of the plant can be soaked in water and its fibres separated and woven to make linen. Linen was more expensive than wool, and was woven in several grades from coarse to fine – fine linen was the most expensive.

> ❖ **ABOUT THE STORY** ❖
>
> *This story does not mean that rich people can't go to heaven. Jesus did not discriminate on the basis of wealth. People who have a lot of possessions tend to focus their life on what they have and can get. God then takes second place in their lives. Jesus said that God had to be first. Sometimes that's easier if you have nothing. You then trust Him for everything.*

The Good Samaritan

Jesus seemed to know the scriptures and the law of Moses so much better than anyone else. The experts who had dedicated their lives to studying God's teachings were jealous of Jesus, and were always trying to catch Him out.

One day, a lawyer came to Jesus to put him to the test. "Teacher, what must I do to win eternal life?" he asked.

"What does the law tell you to do?" Jesus asked.

"It says to love the Lord God with all your heart and soul," the lawyer reeled off pat. "And to love your neighbour as much as you love yourself."

Jesus looked the lawyer firmly in the eye. "Correct," He said. "So there's your answer."

The lawyer wasn't satisfied. "Ah, but who is my neighbour?" he asked smugly.

Jesus answered the question with a story. "A man was travelling from Jerusalem to Jericho," He began, "when bandits attacked him on the road. There was no one around to hear the man's shouts for help. The bandits beat and kicked the man to the ground, until he lay bleeding in the dust. They stripped him of all his possessions and ran off, leaving him for dead."

The lawyer winced at the terrible crime and drew his cloak a little more closely around him.

"Some time later, a priest came along," Jesus went on. "But as soon as the priest saw the dreadfully injured man, he quickly crossed over to the other side of the road and hurried on past, trying not to look."

The lawyer was shocked. How could such a holy man have ignored someone in such need?

"The next traveller to come by was a Levite," Jesus said.

The Levite is sure to help, thought the lawyer. Levites are good people – so good that God rewarded their tribe with the highest positions of office in the temple.

"But the Levite did just the same as the priest," Jesus continued. "He took one look at the naked, bruised body and dashed by on the other side of the road."

The lawyer was appalled. He would have expected such behaviour of a Samaritan – one of the hated people who had taken over Samaria when the Jews were sent to Babylon – but not a Levite!

It was almost as if Jesus had read the lawyer's mind.

Oil flask

In Bible times there were no medicines as we have today. When someone was cut, wine was used to clean the wound. Oil was rubbed on the body to ease pain. This jar would have been used to store olive oil, or possibly wine, in someone's home.

The priest and the Levite

Although the story sounds amazing to us – we would expect religious leaders to help someone – there was a twist in it which Jesus's hearers would have understood. Neither of the leaders would dare touch a dead body, because it would make them "unclean" and unable to do their work for a while. They were thinking of themselves, not caring for their neighbour.

"The third person to see the dying man was a Samaritan," Jesus announced.

Well, that's it then, the lawyer thought, pulling a face. I bet he goes over to see if there's anything to steal and then kicks him when he finds there isn't!

> ❝ *When he saw him, he had compassion.* ❞

Jesus said, loud and clear, "The Samaritan was horrified to see the injured man and rushed over at once to help."

The lawyer couldn't believe his ears!

"The Samaritan cleaned the man's cuts and bandaged the wounds. Then he put the man up on his donkey and went to the nearest town. The Samaritan gave an innkeeper some money to look after the man until he was better. 'If you spend more than that,' the Samaritan told the innkeeper, 'I'll pay you back when I next come this way.' Which of these three travellers would you say was the neighbour of the man who was attacked?" He asked.

"The one who helped him," mumbled the lawyer.

"Yes," said Jesus. "Then go and behave the same way."

I T IS ALWAYS EASIER TO DO WHAT WE WANT THAN TO DO SOMETHING THAT IS BETTER FOR OTHERS, BUT IT IS ALSO COSTLY. THIS STORY TELLS US THAT GOD'S WAY IS SOMETIMES THE HARD WAY.

Lawyers
The lawyers who opposed Jesus were also called "scribes". They were people who copied out the religious law and taught it to others. Jesus said that they had failed to apply their own teaching in the way God intended.

❧ **ABOUT THE STORY** ❧
This parable is probably one of the best known of all of Jesus's stories. People today still talk about a kind person as a "good Samaritan". Jesus wanted people to live out their faith in practical ways. He also implied that we cannot please God just by caring for our neighbour and ignoring God. The two commandments belong together: love God, love others as much as you love yourself.

Joy Over Repentance

FOR centuries, the Jews had always looked up to their religious leaders with the utmost respect. However, these leaders often looked down their noses at the Jewish people.

Jesus's new style of religious leadership was dramatically different. He was often to be found visiting the poor and the sick, laying his hands on lepers or dining at the houses of the hated tax collectors. He not only walked, talked, ate and slept among the common folk, he genuinely seemed to enjoy their company, too. And, in turn, He won vast numbers of their hearts. Jesus never turned anyone away – no matter how lowly their position was in society or how hated they were because of their race or job. Jesus even befriended liars, thieves and vagabonds. Indeed, He often said that He had not been sent to meet good people, but to search out as many sinners as possible.

The Jewish leaders hated Jesus for mingling with those they saw to be the dregs of society. They couldn't understand how a holy man could bring himself to mix with sinners, criminals and down-and-outs. How degrading it was, they thought, to all those who tried hard to uphold the strict religious laws – and degrading most of all, to God.

One day, when a particularly poor crowd had gathered round Jesus to hear the word of God, the Pharisees and scribes began to grumble and complain even more loudly than usual. Jesus soon quietened them by telling a couple of stories.

"A shepherd had a flock of 100 sheep," Jesus began. "But when he came to round them up at the end of the day, he saw that one sheep must have wandered off and got lost. Without a moment's hesitation, the shepherd left his flock in the sheepfold and went off over the fields to look for the one missing sheep. He searched high and low for a

❖ ABOUT THE STORY ❖

Jesus taught that every human being has dignity before God. Indeed, the whole Bible teaches that. People at the bottom of the social pile, and despised by others, are said to be of special concern to God. In these stories, Jesus shows that God actively looks for people who need Him and lavishes His love on them, even if they have done wrong in the past.

Silver ingots
In Old Testament times, people used silver ingots like this as money. The value depended on the weight. By New Testament times this was becoming less common for everyday trading, as there were many coins in circulation.

Beer jug
Most of the people Jesus met drank wine which was cheap and easy to make from the grapes grown locally. Beer was not widely drunk in Palestine. This beer jug is unusual and perhaps belonged to a rich person.

long time, and when he finally heard a lonely bleating he was overjoyed. The shepherd returned home with the stray animal, knocking on all his friends' and neighbours' doors to share the good news with them.

"And there was a woman who owned ten pieces of silver. Then, one night, one of them went missing. Determined to find it, she lit a lamp and searched through the house, sweeping every nook and cranny, turning out every corner and cupboard, shifting every piece of furniture, until she found it. 'Hooray!' she cried to her friends and neighbours. 'I have found my lost piece of silver!' And they all celebrated with her."

At first, the disgruntled Pharisees and scribes were puzzled at the stories. They didn't see what lost sheep, or a woman losing her money, had to do with them. But their faces grew red with embarrassment when they heard Jesus's explanation.

> ❝ *Just so, I tell you, there is joy before the angels of God over one sinner who repents.* ❞

"Like the shepherd's joy over his one lost sheep, there will be more gladness in heaven over one sinner who repents than there will be over 99 good people who do not need any forgiveness. And like the woman's happiness at finding her single piece of silver, there will be great celebrations in heaven for each and every sinner who repents – no matter how common or humble they are."

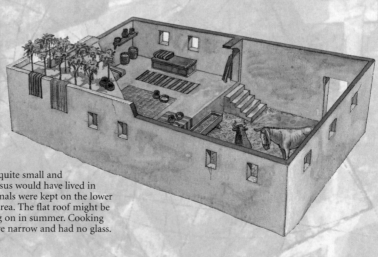

I**T IS VERY EASY TO LOOK DOWN ON PEOPLE WHO ARE LESS WELL OFF THAN US OR WHO HAVE "STRAYED" FROM GOD'S WAYS. CHRISTIANS ARE CALLED TO LOVE SUCH PEOPLE JUST AS GOD LOVES THEM.** ∼

Palestinian house
Most houses in New Testament times were quite small and often only had one room (on two levels). Jesus would have lived in such a house, and visited many others. Animals were kept on the lower level; the family ate and slept in the raised area. The flat roof might be used for drying crops or eating and sleeping on in summer. Cooking was usually done outside. The windows were narrow and had no glass.

The Story of the Prodigal Son

JESUS had a powerful parable for the snooty religious elders about showing forgiveness to sinners. "Once upon a time," He began, "there lived a wealthy farmer. He had two sons who worked beside him on the land and he was content that they would inherit the farm when he died and would look after it well. However, one day the younger son came to him with a proposition.

"'Father, I'm old enough now to choose my own path,' the lad said, 'and I want to go off and see the world.' He shifted about from foot to foot, looked down at the floor and nervously cleared his throat. 'I was hoping you could perhaps give me my share of the farm now, in cash.'

"The farmer was more than a bit taken aback by this unusual request but, being a generous man who loved his sons dearly, he agreed. And as soon as the money was in the younger son's hand, he packed his bags and set off, looking for excitement and adventure.

"Unfortunately, the lad wasn't as mature and capable as he had thought. He managed to travel a long way, saw lots of sights and eventually made it safely to a distant city. But there he fell in with a bad lot of friends, who were only too willing to help him squander his money. Before long, the boy found his purse was empty. Of course, the moment the farmer's son hit hard times his "friends" disappeared. He found himself alone and penniless.

"He knew there was nothing else for it but to try to find a job. However, a dreadful famine suddenly swept the country and everyone tightened their belts. It was no good begging for scraps or rooting for leftovers – there weren't any.

And the only work the boy knew how to do – farming the land – was scarce. The desperate young man was thankful to get a job as a lowly swineherd.

"Every day as the farmer's son drove the pigs out to feed, he had to fight off the urge to eat some of the pigswill for himself. He was miserable and starving.

"'On my father's farm even the hired hands have enough to eat,' he moaned to himself, 'and they still have food left over. Why, oh why did I leave home!'

"Bit by bit, the lad swallowed his pride.

"'I want to go home,' he finally decided. 'I'll go back to my father and beg his forgiveness for being such an arrogant fool. I won't even dare ask him to accept me back as his son, but perhaps he'll take me back as one of his labourers – and that's more than I deserve.'

"The farmer's head had been filled with thoughts of his son every single day he had been away. He had worried over him and missed him, and hadn't stopped loving him for one second. When the landowner saw his child's familiar figure approaching from the distance he ran to meet him as fast as his ageing legs would carry him.

> **Father, I have sinned and I am no longer worthy to be called your son.**

"'Father,' the trembling boy wept, as his father enveloped him in a huge bear-hug. 'I have sinned against God and against you. I am no longer worthy to be called your son.'

"'Bring out my best robes!' the farmer interrupted, calling to his servants. 'Dress my son in my best clothes! Put my ring on his hand and new shoes on his feet! Bring that calf we were saving for a festival and cook it up into something really special! We're going to celebrate and feast like never before. My long lost son has come home!'

"While the younger son was filled with repentance and gratitude, his older brother was furious.

"'Father, what do you mean by all this?' he demanded angrily. 'How am I supposed to feel? I have stayed here and worked with you all these years and you've never thrown a feast for me! But as soon as this loser shows up again, having wasted all your hard-earned money, you give him the best of everything you own!'

"With tears of joy in his eyes, the farmer took his eldest son by the hand.

"'Son, you don't know how much it means to me that you have remained by my side. And everything I have is yours. But today is a day to be glad. For your brother was dead to me and now he is alive; he was lost and now we have found him again!'"

Ploughshare

Today, ploughs have steel "shares", the part that digs into the earth and turns it over. In ancient times they probably had iron blades which were fixed to the forked branch of a tree. Ploughs were pulled by oxen, often yoked together in pairs. The farmer walked behind, steering the plough by the handle. Ploughing was essential to preparing hard soil for the seed.

Signet ring

The ring given by the father to his son was probably like this one, a signet ring. It might have had a family symbol on it. It was a sign of authority and honour, rather than being just a piece of jewellery. Rings were commonly worn by both men and women in Biblical times.

❧ ABOUT THE STORY ❧

This moving story is not really about the son at all, but about his father. The older man is always looking for the boy, and when he comes at last, the father is ready to forgive and forget his sins. Jesus meant that as a picture of God. He wants people to come back humbly to Him, and He will forgive what ever they have done that is wrong.

Heaven and Hell

ALTHOUGH Jesus spoke often about the coming kingdom of God, many people didn't understand what He meant. They thought of the great rulers of the time who had magnificent palaces of gold and silver, treasure houses full of jewels, armies of golden chariots and armoured footsoldiers, and ranks of slaves to do their bidding. They pictured Jesus as the proclaimed king of the Jews and at the head of a mighty army, which would come marching through Judea, flags flying, to take charge of the country. The Pharisees once challenged, "So when is the kingdom of God coming, then?"

Jesus replied, "The kingdom of God will not come with great announcements and fanfares, nor will there be anything splendid to see. For the kingdom of God is inside you." Jesus was talking about a spiritual kingdom that exists through life and after death, where both good and wickedness will grow until the end of time. Then God will cast out everything that is evil, leaving only goodness.

As well as not understanding what the kingdom was like, it was also difficult for people to accept Jesus's teachings on what they had to do to enter it.

"Everybody wants lots of money, a big house, an important job and expensive possessions, don't they?" they would wonder. "But Jesus tells us that none of these things are important in the kingdom of God – in fact, they can even stop you getting there!"

> ❝ *And at his gate lay a poor man named Lazarus.* ❞

"Yes," others would agree. "Jesus says that if we want to enter the kingdom, instead of envying those who have lots of servants, we should give our lives willingly to helping others. Instead of trying to get rich, we should give away everything we own to those who are poor."

One day, Jesus told the people a story that He hoped would help them understand before it was too late. "There was once a very rich man who lived in a huge house. Every day he dressed in the finest clothes and dined at a table overflowing with the best food. Each day a wretched beggar called Lazarus would crouch outside the gates of the mansion, dreaming of what it would be like to taste

A triumphant emperor
This is the sort of leader many people expected Jesus to be, a commander of an army riding into a city in a triumphant procession, such as the Roman emperor shown above. Instead Jesus came meekly, riding on a donkey.

Riches
These are Roman coins from the first century. The rich man was so greedy that he didn't think about God at all, and ended up separated from God in hell.

Judea
Judea was the name that the Romans gave to the area that the Jews called Judah. It was ruled by a Roman governor until after Jesus's death.

some of the rich man's leftovers. Lazarus was all alone, starving and in rags. He was so miserable he barely noticed the stray dogs who licked his filthy skin, or the flies that crawled over his skinny body.

"Eventually, the poor man's suffering came to an end and he died. And as he left the dirt and poverty of his life in this world, angels hurried to carry his soul to heaven.

"Now it so happened that soon afterwards the rich man died as well – but his soul was taken straight to the fires of hell. As he suffered in torment, the rich man cast his eyes heavenwards and saw the beggar standing side by side with the great Abraham, father of the Jewish people.

"'Abraham!' the rich man screamed. 'Have mercy on me and send Lazarus to cool my burning tongue with a few drops of water! I am being burnt alive!'

"Abraham remained unmoved and his voice was stern.

"'Son, remember that on earth you surrounded yourself with luxury and comfort, leaving Lazarus in the cold. Now he is being comforted while you suffer. Besides, it's impossible for those in heaven to be cast into hell, and for those in hell to escape to heaven. Hell is an eternal punishment.'

"The rich man groaned in despair. Too late, he began to think of other people.

"'Then please at least send Lazarus to my father's house. I have five brothers and they're all like me. They need warning, or they'll all end up here!'

"Abraham shook his head.

"'No!' he bellowed. 'They have the words of Moses and the prophets. If they don't heed those great people, they won't take notice of any other voice from the dead.'"

WE CANNOT EXPECT GOD TO GIVE US GOOD THINGS IF WE NEVER SHARE OUR GOOD THINGS WITH OTHERS. IN FACT, IF WE DON'T LEARN TO GIVE, WE WILL BECOME GREEDY AND SHUT OFF FROM GOD'S LOVE.

Dogs
In New Testament times, Jews did not have dogs as pets. They roamed the streets and scavenged scraps. They regarded them as vermin and "unclean". So being licked by dogs made Lazarus a complete outcast in Jewish eyes.

❖ ABOUT THE STORY ❖

This story is about having right attitudes to money and people in this life. It refers to life after death in the popular terms of the day. It is not intended to teach us more about eternity than that some people go to be with God and others don't. It does show that we "reap" in the next life what we "sow" in this one, however. It encouraged Jesus's hearers that God loves those who are despised.

Opposition to Jesus Grows

JESUS'S preaching was sometimes so bold that it outraged many of the Jews.

"He says to us, 'I have come down from heaven'. How dare He!" many of them exclaimed. "This is just Jesus, after all, the son of Mary and Joseph!"

"He says to us, 'I am the living bread from heaven'!" others scoffed. "What on earth does He mean?"

Even some of Jesus's faithful followers were offended when He said, "He who eats my flesh and drinks my blood has eternal life, and I will raise him up on the last day."

"It's the spirit that's important," Jesus explained, "not the flesh that surrounds it. My words promise life."

After this, many of Jesus's disciples gave up in disgust.

"What about you?" Jesus asked His 12 closest friends. "Do you want to leave me too?"

Peter spoke up determinedly for all the disciples.

"No, Lord," he reassured Jesus. "You speak to us of how to win eternal life and we believe you. We have all come to know that you are God's Chosen One."

> **66** *The chief priests and Pharisees sent officers to arrest Him.* **99**

"Yes, and *I* chose you," Jesus reminded them. "But I have to tell you, one of you will turn to evil."

The disciples were shocked, but Jesus would say no more.

By the time of the feast of Tabernacles, Jesus had

❖ ABOUT THE STORY ❖

What made life difficult for the religious leaders was that Jesus was not denying the laws of Moses. He was thinking about them and applying them in a different way. Jesus showed people that the law without love was of no value. He did not break the law but applied it more thoughtfully and more fairly than the harsh and uncaring ways of the Pharisees.

Soldiers

Roman soldiers were based in Judea to keep the peace. The chief priests also had their own guards and it was probably these who tried to arrest Jesus. However, it was the Romans who finally crucified Him.

∼ARMOUR OF GOD ∼

The apostle Paul described to early Christians the armour that they would need to fight the power of the devil. He described it to them as if it were the armour of a Roman soldier.

Equipment	Meaning
Belt	Truth
Breastplate	Righteousness
Sandals	Gospel of peace
Shield	Faith
Helmet	Salvation
Sword of the Spirit	Word of God

offended so many of the elders that going publicly to Jerusalem was highly dangerous. But he was determined to celebrate the occasion properly. When the news spread that Jesus, a wanted man, was preaching openly in the temple, the Jews were amazed.

The chief priests and the Pharisees ordered his immediate arrest as a rabble-rouser. But the officers came back empty-handed.

"Where is He?" cried the chief priests and Pharisees. "Why haven't you brought Him to us?"

"He's an extraordinary man!" the officers answered sheepishly. "We've never heard anyone speak like Him. The crowds love Him. Everyone's talking about Him and wondering what He means! But even though He speaks strangely, He hasn't done anything wrong. What can we arrest Him for?"

The chief priests and Pharisees decided they'd have to trick Jesus into openly defying one of the laws and then He'd *have* to be arrested.

Next day, Jesus was teaching in the temple when the scribes, priests and Pharisees strode in to talk to Him.

"Teacher," they said to Jesus, dragging forward a frightened woman. "This woman is a sinner. She has been seen with another woman's husband. Now, the law of Moses says she should be stoned to death. What do you think we should do with her?"

Jesus stood up and faced the hostile officials. "Let he who has never sinned throw the first stone," He said.

Jesus's answer completely thwarted the authorities. He hadn't interpreted the law of Moses as they did, but His answer hadn't broken it either. After all, all of them had sinned in some way; they were only human. Lost for words, they stormed out.

Holy Communion
In this service, Christians eat bread and drink wine, which symbolize Jesus's body and blood, reminding people of Jesus's death on the cross for their sins.

Pens
These pens come from Roman times and may have been the sort used by the scribes in Judea. Scribes wrote letters for people and also copied the scriptures.

Bull sacrifice
The Jews sacrificed a bull in the temple once a year to show they were sorry for their sins. The New Testament says that 'the blood of bulls' cannot take away people's sins; only Jesus can do that.

Ungrateful Lepers

WHEREVER Jesus went, His fame as a healer spread before Him. One day ten figures, tattered and mishapen, stumbled into the path ahead. They stood a little way off and held up their hands. The disciples realized that the group was infected with leprosy.

"Jesus, master, have mercy on us," they moaned.

"Go and show yourselves to the priest," Jesus said.

Filled with hope, they did what He told them. The lepers hadn't gone far when they felt their skin tingle. They looked at each other in disbelief. Trembling, they felt the smoothness of their skin. They were cured! Weeping tears of happiness, they ripped off their bandages and danced with joy. They were cured!

" *Then said Jesus, 'Were not ten cleansed? Where are the nine?'* **"**

Some time later, Jesus and His disciples saw a stranger running towards them.

"Thanks be to God who healed me!" the man wept.

The astonished disciples realized he was one of the lepers, now totally cured.

"You're a Samaritan, aren't you?" said Jesus. "Tell me, where are the other nine I healed? Are you the only one who's come back to give thanks and praise God?"

❧ ABOUT THE STORY ❧

When the man came back, Jesus told him that his faith had made him well, that is "whole". He was healed not only in his body but in his spirit because he had come to worship God. Jesus healed people because He cared about their physical needs. But He also cared about their spiritual requirements and their life as a whole.

Lourdes
Healing is a mysterious thing. Even doctors don't always know why some people get better and others don't. Christians believe that people who are ill should pray for God's healing as well as go to doctors. Some make pilgrimages to special places such as Lourdes (seen here) where they believe God sometimes performs special miracles of healing.

The Power of Prayer

JESUS often said how important it was to pray – and He didn't just mean reciting long verses in the temple. He meant having private conversations with God about everyday worries and asking for personal guidance. This was a new idea for many people.

"If your child asked you for a fish or an egg to eat, would you give them a snake or a scorpion?" He said. "Of course not! Well, if you give good gifts to your children, think about all the wonderful things your heavenly Father knows how to give you if you only ask Him!"

> " *And He told them a parable, to the effect that they ought always to pray and not lose heart.* "

Jesus realised that some people would misunderstand Him, and would expect to pray for something one day and have it the next. So He told a story to show that people should never stop talking to God, even if they felt their prayers weren't being answered.

"There was once an arrogant judge who had no respect for either God or people. He simply didn't care if justice was being done or not. However, every day a good woman would come to his house and bang on the door.

"'I am being wronged by my neighbour!' she would yell. 'Please come with me and consider the case, then you can give me a just verdict.'

"Day after day the judge ignored her. But she still turned up. 'She's never going to give up!' the judge finally burst out. 'She's going to plague me for ever!' And he went and sorted out her problem for her – just so she wouldn't bother him again."

Jesus told His disciples, "The woman was so determined that even the corrupt judge gave her what she wanted. So imagine how much faster the heavenly Father will respond to the pleas of those He cares for."

Votive hand
The Romans often sought healing by visiting the temple of their favourite god. They would make offerings to the god and say a prayer. Sometimes they would leave a model of the part of the body they wanted to be healed, such as this hand. This was called a votive offering. Some people left models of ears, which we assume was because they were deaf.

Physician and child
On this marble tombstone a doctor is seen examining a child. Medicine in the first century was very crude. On the ground is a cup for collecting blood, possibly taken to try to cure the child.

❧ ABOUT THE STORY ❧
Jesus taught that prayer isn't about trying to make God do what we want Him to do, but about finding out what God wants us to do. Jesus showed that God always wants the best for people, that is by getting to know and trust God even when life is difficult. God may know that wealth or healing is best for someone, but Jesus didn't promise that either were ours by right.

The Pharisee and the Tax Collector

THE Pharisees had been brought up from birth to think that they were special – different from common Jews and way above the likes of foreigners. And none of the lessons that Jesus taught through His stories managed to get through to them. The Pharisees took great pride in the way in which they carefully observed every single rule of the faith, and it blinded their eyes, sealed their ears, closed their minds and hardened their hearts. When Jesus preached how good people should befriend sinners and forgive them, the Pharisees merely scoffed. When Jesus taught that the wealthy should give all they had to the poor – even if they were ungodly, undeserving people – the Pharisees just sneered. It was impossible to shake their confidence in the righteousness of their own beliefs and habits.

Still, even though the Pharisees were Jesus's worst enemies, He never gave up trying to warn them about how they were falling unwittingly into sin.

"Once upon a time," He told His disciples, "two men went into the temple to pray. One was a Pharisee..."

The Pharisees in the crowd looked smug. How good we are, they thought, making sure we pray at all the right times!

"The other man was a tax collector," Jesus went on.

The Pharisees bristled. How dare a Roman-loving traitor venture into the holy temple before God, they thought.

Jesus saw the Pharisees' self-satisfied faces change to looks of disgust, but He went on regardless.

"The Pharisee strode straight into the centre of the temple, in full view of everyone. He made a great, solemn show of lifting his eyes and arms up towards heaven and then he began to pray out loud.

Ceremonial washing
Jewish rituals in the first century often involved ceremonial washings as a symbol of being cleansed from sin. There was a large laver bowl in the temple, and probably smaller ones like this were used both in the temple and elsewhere. Jesus taught that people needed to purify their hearts, not their hands, if they were to know God, and that meant doing God's will and not just performing ceremonies.

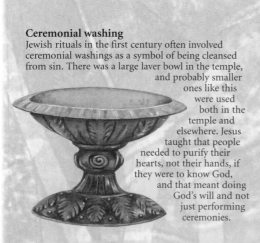

Roman gods
The Romans who had invaded Judea worshipped many gods, although they did not build temples to them in Judea and the Jews were not especially aware of them. Later, Christians encountered them a great deal. Jupiter (far left) was the king of the sky and god of thunderstorms. Minerva (left) was the patron goddess of craft and wisdom. She was also the patron goddess of the Emperor Domitian, who persecuted Christians.

'God, thank you for making me different from everyone else,' he announced. 'Thank you for lifting me above all the liars, thieves and scoundrels. I fast twice a week, I give a percentage of all I earn to charity and I'm glad about it. God, thank you for making me better than people like that no-good tax collector who crept in with me,' he cried.

"The tax collector was hiding behind a pillar in the furthest, darkest corner of the temple. He didn't dare venture out where anyone might see him. He hung his head and wrung his hands. His heart was heavy with the anguish of wrongdoing and the burden of regret.

"'Oh Lord, I am a sinner,' he whispered, looking at the floor in shame. 'I beg you to have mercy on me.'"

> " *But the tax collector would not even lift up his eyes to heaven.* "

Jesus paused for a moment and looked round at the waiting faces of the crowd. He saw that the Pharisees were scowling, angry at how he had portrayed them as pompous, conceited windbags to everyone that was listening. But nevertheless, He looked them straight in the eye and He finished the story.

"I tell you, that day it was the tax collector who went home blessed by the Lord," Jesus said. "For all those who set themselves high will eventually fall, and all those who consider themselves lowly will be raised up."

The Pharisees stood up, fuming with cold rage. They turned on their heels and stalked off, their elaborate robes swirling out behind them.

Animal sacrifices
Many ancient religions offered sacrifices of animals. The Romans did it only occasionally, but butchers often slaughtered meat using special pagan ceremonies, and this caused the first Christians real problems of conscience. This sacrificial knife would have been used to slit animals' throats. It has an ornate lion's head on the handle.

Seat of Moses
Synagogues often had a stone seat at the front called the "Seat of Moses" .The scribe who taught the law of Moses sat there, and in a sense was sitting in Moses's place. This ancient seat was found in a synagogue in Chorazin, in Galilee.

> ❖ **ABOUT THE STORY** ❖
>
> *This is an important parable because the attitude of the Pharisee is one which still exists in our society today. Jesus is saying that it doesn't matter how good a particular person is, they can never be good enough for God. This is because everyone has sinned in some way. Jesus told people not to compare themselves with others, but with God instead.*

Martha and Mary

JESUS and His disciples were gradually drawing nearer to the capital city, Jerusalem. The 12 friends brooded on the awful things Jesus had told them would happen to Him when He got there.

One of the villages Jesus stopped at on His way to Jerusalem was Bethany. A woman named Martha invited Jesus to come and stay at her house.

Martha made sure that Jesus and His friends were cool and comfortable, and at once set about serving the weary people with refreshments. As she bustled in and out, carrying in jugs of wine, pitchers of water, drinking goblets and plates of nibbles, another young woman crept out of an inner room and quietly sat down.

> 66 *Mary sat at the Lord's feet and listened to His teaching.* 99

"Mary, come and give me a hand!" Martha hissed at her sister, as she deposited another tray of food among the hungry guests. But Mary just shrugged and turned back to

Jesus, listening intently to every word He had to say.

Martha stood there, hands on hips, more than a little bit annoyed. She too would like to sit with the great preacher and chat. But if she did that, everyone would be left hungry and thirsty. After all, someone had to get the

dinner... The dinner! She remembered with a shock the pot she had left boiling over the flames and hurried back to attend to it.

Martha made trip after trip to and from the kitchen, carrying in course after course of delicious food and taking out load after load of empty cups and plates. When the final morsel was laid on the table, she went to join Jesus and His friends. But how left out Martha felt by then! The disciples were deep in a conversation she couldn't follow; she had no idea what they were talking about or laughing at. And there was scarcely room for her to sit down at the very edge of the group!

Martha had been determined to show Jesus and His friends the very best hospitality she could provide – but in doing so she'd hardly seen anything of the great preacher she so admired. She looked at her lazy sister sitting there at Jesus's feet, gazing up at Him in awe! Martha's face was flushed, her arms were aching and now her lip began to tremble.

"Lord!" she burst out sobbing. "Don't you care that my sister has left me to do everything? Why don't you tell her to get up and help me?"

While Mary hung her head in shame and the disciples fell into an embarrassed silence, Jesus got up to comfort the poor woman.

"Martha, Martha," he soothed, "you have

concerned yourself with preparing and cooking all these different dishes when we only needed one to satisfy our hunger. Your sister has chosen the best dish of all – listening to me   and it will not be taken away from her."

Tableware

Romans in the first century used elaborate plates and cups at their meal tables, although the Jews tended to use plainer ones. The potter was an important person in every town, because everyone needed his wares. Cups generally didn't have handles. There were no knives or forks, either – Jesus and His friends would have picked food out of dishes and eaten it with their fingers.

Bethany

Bethany was a small village about 3km (5 miles) east of Jerusalem, towards Jericho. Jesus seems to have stayed here quite often and was very close to Mary, Martha and their brother Lazarus. This painting, found in a church in Bethany, shows Jesus raising Lazarus from the dead.

❖ ABOUT THE STORY ❖

Jesus is gently teaching Martha about priorities. She thinks that the most important thing is to entertain her guests, but it stopped her from learning about God through Jesus's teaching. She wasted a unique opportunity to be fed spiritually, because she was too concerned about physical food. Jesus taught that God was more important than food because life with Him lasted for ever.

Lazarus is Brought Back to Life

MARTHA and Mary had a brother, Lazarus, and they all became firm friends with Jesus. But the time soon came for Him to move on once again.

Some weeks later Jesus was preaching and healing far away when a messenger came to Him with an urgent request.

"Lazarus is seriously ill," the messenger explained, "so ill that Martha and Mary fear he is dying. They beg you to come as quickly as you can to make him well again."

The disciples knew how fond Jesus was of the family and expected Him to drop everything and hurry off. To their surprise, Jesus just remarked, "This will not end in Lazarus's death. He has been struck down as a way for God to show His glory through me." And Jesus calmly stayed where He was, continuing His work.

Two days later Jesus announced that He was heading back to Bethany. But the disciples were worried.

"Master, you have many enemies there," they said. "Some people have even sworn to stone you! Surely you shouldn't go back there."

"It is not time yet for my life to end. I will be safe for the moment," Jesus replied. "Now our friend Lazarus has fallen asleep and I must go and wake him."

"Lord, if he is sleeping, he will wake up on his own," the disciples protested, not quite understanding.

"Lazarus is dead," Jesus sighed, "and I am glad that I was not there when he died. Because of this, your belief in me will grow." Jesus smiled at His bewildered followers. "Now let's forget these fears and go to him right away."

By the time Jesus arrived at Bethany, Lazarus had been dead for four days. A pale-faced Martha came out of the village to meet Him.

"If only you had been here, Lord, my brother would not have died," said Martha, her voice cracking. "But I know that God will do anything you ask."

Jesus was filled with compassion at Martha's faith.

He said to her, "I am the resurrection and the life.

❧ ABOUT THE STORY ❧

This was not only one of Jesus's greatest miracles, it was also a great teaching moment too. When He wept, Jesus showed how ugly and wrong death is, and how much it grieved Him. When He spoke to Martha, He showed that He was the God who could control life and death. And when He called Lazarus out, He showed that the power of God is absolute.

Sarcophagi
This is an elaborate stone coffin. Only a few rich people in Judea were buried in them, however. Most dead bodies, including Lazarus and later Jesus, were wrapped up in bandages and placed on a ledge or on the floor of a natural cave or tomb cut out of a rocky hillside.

Sleeping
Jesus said that Lazarus was not dead, only sleeping, an image often used in the Bible. Jesus uses this image to teach His disciples that physical death is not the end, but leads to a new spiritual life.

Anyone who believes in me and dies will live again, and anyone who believes in me and lives will never die." He held Martha's gaze. "Do you believe this?" He asked.

"Yes, Lord," Martha whispered in awe. "I believe that you are the Christ, the Son of God." And she ran back to the house to fetch her sister.

As Jesus watched Mary and her grief-stricken friends, a shadow clouded His face. Mary fell at Jesus's feet and sobbed as if her heart was breaking.

Jesus asked her gently, "Where have you buried him?"

And as Jesus was shown the way to Lazarus's tomb, He too broke down and wept for His dear friend.

Lazarus had been laid in a cave, with a large rock rolled across the entrance to keep out wild beasts or bandits.

Jesus's voice was low and firm.

"Take away the stone," He ordered.

Martha gave a little gasp. "Lord, he has been dead for four days now. His corpse will smell."

"Didn't I promise you that if you only believe, you will see the glory of God?" Jesus replied. "Roll away the stone."

As Martha and Mary's friends began to heave the huge rock, Jesus began to pray.

"Father, I thank you for hearing my voice," he said. "I know that you always hear me. But I want everyone here to know and believe that it is you who sent me."

The friends heaved one last time and the rock moved aside. Jesus took a step forward and shouted into the gloomy interior.

"Lazarus!" His voice echoed. "Come out!"

No one moved a muscle.

All was perfectly still and silent.

And then they heard the sound of muffled footsteps coming towards them from the depths of the cave, and the dead man came slowly walking out into the sunlight, all wrapped up in a shroud. He stopped in front of Jesus.

> **The dead man came out, his face wrapped with a cloth.**

"Unbind him," Jesus ordered, "and let him go."
And the overjoyed Martha and Mary did just that.

Tomb of Lazarus
Many years after New Testament times, people built this monument to Lazarus at the place in Bethany where they think his tomb was.

The Story of the Unmerciful Servant

MOST of the astonished men and women who had seen Lazarus walking out of his tomb believed they had witnessed a miracle. However, a few troublemakers thought it was a trick. They hurried to the chief priests and Pharisees, calling an emergency council meeting at once.

"What on earth are we going to do?" they grumbled. "It doesn't really matter whether He's genuine or not. If we let Him keep on like this, soon everyone in Judea will believe in Him. The Romans will think that there's a serious threat, crush the whole nation and destroy our religion."

The high priest Caiaphas had a different opinion.

"This Jesus will die for the good of us all," he prophesied. The chief priests and Pharisees wouldn't listen. From that moment on, they made up their minds that it was more important than ever to find a way to have Jesus put to death.

Jesus was well aware that He wasn't liked by everybody, but He always preached that people should forgive their enemies, such as the time when Peter came to him with an important question.

"Lord, how many times should I forgive someone who does me wrong?" Peter asked. "Up to seven times?"

Jesus replied, "Not just seven, but seventy-seven – forgive them every single time." And he told a story to explain why.

"There was once a generous king who had kindly lent money to several of his servants. The time came for the servants to repay their debts, and the king called them in, one by one. One servant in particular had borrowed a vast

sum of money – ten thousand talents, in total. And when it was this servant's turn, he stood in front of the king ashen-faced, his knees knocking. He had failed to make enough money to pay back what he owed.

"The king followed the terms of the contract and ordered that the loan should be made good by selling the servant, his wife and his children into slavery, and auctioning all of his possessions. The devastated man fell on his knees, sobbing and begging forgiveness.

"'My lord!' he cried. 'Have mercy on me! Bear with me a little while longer and I promise I will find every last penny that I owe you.'

"The good king took pity on the poor man and agreed to give him some more time to pay. Trembling with relief at his narrow escape, the servant rushed from the throne room. As he left the palace, he came across one of his

Prisoners go to work
This ancient stone relief shows prisoners handcuffed to each other and escorted by guards. They may be going to work. Most prisoners in ancient times worked in labour camps rather than being kept in jails.

Restraint
When prisoners were kept in a jail, they were usually shackled in some way. Having their feet locked in a kind of "stocks" was the most common form of restraint. Sometimes prisoners were chained to their guard to stop them escaping.

work colleagues, a man who owed him the rather small amount of one hundred denarii. The servant was desperate. Grabbing his frightened friend around the throat, he pushed the man up against the wall and threatened him. 'Give me my money!' the servant demanded. 'I need it now – or else!' Just as the servant had done, the man broke down and begged for more time to pay. The servant was ruthless. He had the man immediately flung into prison until he found a way to come up with the money.

"When the other palace employees heard about the servant's behaviour, they went to tell the king. Soon, the cruel man found himself back in the throne room. This time, the king wasn't smiling, he was frowning angrily.

"'You wicked servant!' the king roared. 'You begged me to be merciful, to not sell your belongings and put you in prison, and I gave you more time to repay your debt. Don't you think you should have shown similar forgiveness to your friend?' And the king had the hard-hearted servant thrown into jail at once."

> 66 *Should not you have had mercy on your fellow servant, as I had mercy on you?* 99

Jesus explained what the parable meant. "The king is like my heavenly Father," he said. "And if you don't find it in your heart to forgive people, your punishment will be the same as the unmerciful servant's."

THE UNFORGIVING SERVANT WAS SELFISH. HE GRABBED HIS OWN FREEDOM BUT DENIED SOMEONE ELSE THEIRS. JESUS USED THIS AS AN EXAMPLE TO SHOW THAT PEOPLE SHOULD BE KIND TO EACH OTHER. ∾

Forgiveness
This painting of Jesus offering forgiveness and a welcome into heaven reminds people that any sin is a sin against God. The New Testament teaches that forgiveness is offered freely by God as an act of grace.

✣ ABOUT THE STORY ✣

In this story Jesus wants His listeners to see how great God's forgiveness is, and to learn to treat each other as God treats them. It is hypocritical to accept His forgiveness yet not offer it to others, because people who love God are called to imitate His ways in their lives. Indeed, if people did not forgive each other, Jesus warned, they would be unable to appreciate what God had done for them.

Zaccheus is Forgiven

ZACCHEUS was a fat little man. A fat little man whom nobody liked very much. For Zaccheus was Jericho's chief tax collector. And by collecting his countrymen's hard-earned money for the hated Romans – and taking extra for himself – he had made himself very rich.

"Here comes that traitor, Zaccheus," people would say as they saw him walking down the road, and they'd cross over to the other side of the street.

"Here comes that crook, Zaccheus," people would sneer as they saw him out shopping, and they'd shut up their market stalls to avoid serving him.

"Here comes that liar, Zaccheus," people would whisper as they saw him entering the synagogue to pray, and they'd turn their backs as he went past.

All Zaccheus's ill-gotten wealth couldn't make up for the hatred people felt towards him and for the loneliness of his life.

Just like all the other citizens of Jericho, for many months now Zaccheus had heard stories of an amazing holy man called Jesus of Nazareth, who preached the most inspiring sermons and performed miracles of healing. And when Zaccheus heard people gossiping outside his window of how Jesus would be passing through Jericho that very day, Zaccheus was determined not to miss the opportunity to see Him. He locked up the tax office at once and went out into the street. It wasn't difficult to work out where Jesus was going to be. He could already hear a buzz of excitement coming from the other side of the city. Zaccheus hurried off at once, as fast as his short legs would carry him.

By the time Zaccheus reached the route that Jesus was expected to take, crowds of people had already lined the streets – ten or twelve people thick in places. Zaccheus jumped up and down, trying to see over their shoulders, but he was too small. All he could see was row

upon row of the back of people's heads. So Zaccheus tried pushing. He set his shoulder to the jostling wall of bodies in front of him and heaved, trying to squeeze through. All he got was his toes stamped on and an elbow in the eye. He was just as shut out of the ranks as before.

Then Zaccheus had an idea. Huffing and puffing in the hot noonday sun, he set off again running – right down the pavement behind all the crowds. Hurry, hurry, he thought to himself. Hurry or you might miss him. Zaccheus didn't quite know why he wanted to see Jesus so much, but he knew he did. He realized with surprise that nothing else would have got him running so fast through the streets of Jericho.

> **❝** *And he sought to see who Jesus was, but could not because he was small of stature.* **❞**

Just when Zaccheus thought that his legs were going to give way and his heart was going to burst inside his chest, he reached what he was looking for – a tall, thick sycamore tree that he used to climb as a boy. Come on, Zaccheus, the panting chief tax collector thought to himself, you can still do it if you put your mind to it. And he reached up on tiptoe into its branches.

How everyone would have laughed if they had seen the fat man scrambling up the tree trunk in a most undignified way. No one was taking any notice. They were far too intent on peering into the distance to catch the first glimpse of Jesus coming down the road.

As Zacchaeus balanced himself uncomfortably among the branches, the crowd began to cheer and jump up and down. Way above their heads, Zacchaeus could see everything. Making their way slowly through the clamouring, grabbing people was a group of very simply-dressed men. And in the middle of them was a man with the kindest face he had ever seen.

Zacchaeus knew he had to be Jesus of Nazareth. The way Jesus smiled so gently at the noisy rabble all around Him made Zacchaeus feel truly ashamed of the swindling he had done in the past, and he longed to jump straight down from the tree and join him.

Jesus was drawing nearer and nearer, until He was right underneath Zacchaeus's sycamore tree. And the chief tax collector nearly fell off his perch with shock, for Jesus suddenly stopped, peered up through the leaves right at him and said his name.

"Zacchaeus, hurry up and come down," Jesus said. "I'm on my way to stay with you."

The crowd fell silent. They weren't just amazed to see Zacchaeus the chief tax collector nesting in a tree, they were also stunned that the holy man had even lowered Himself to speak to him – let alone say that He wanted to visit his house.

"What about us?" they began to murmur. "Why does the preacher want to go and stay with a nasty man like that?"

The delighted Zacchaeus didn't give them a chance to persuade Jesus to change His mind. The little man leapt out of the tree and bowed down before Jesus.

"Lord," Zacchaeus said, "you know that I am a sinner. However I stand before you today a changed man. I intend to give half of everything I own to the poor. And I'm going to look back through my records and give anyone that I've ever cheated four times as much as I owe them."

Jesus smiled and laid His hand on Zacchaeus's arm. "I have come to find people just like you," He said.

With that Zacchaeus eagerly escorted Jesus to his house.

Jericho
Zacchaeus lived in Jericho, believed to be the oldest walled town in the world. This plaster-covered skull dates from about 7000BC. It was made when the people of Jericho prayed to their ancestors.

PEOPLE WERE AMAZED THAT JESUS SHOULD TAKE ANY NOTICE OF A BAD PERSON SUCH AS ZACCHAEUS. BUT JESUS SHOWED THAT BAD PEOPLE OFTEN WANT TO BE LOVED AND ACCEPTED, AND THAT WHEN THEY ARE, THEY CAN CHANGE FOR THE BETTER WITH GOD'S HELP. HE CALLED HIS FOLLOWERS TO LOVE AND ACCEPT OTHERS, AND NOT TO JUDGE THEM

⌖ ABOUT THE STORY ⌖

Zacchaeus responded to Jesus with great generosity because he appreciated his forgiveness. The Jewish law said that a thief should pay back twice what he had taken, but Zacchaeus paid back four times as much. This is an example of "repentance": showing our sorrow by what we do. It was a sign that Zacchaeus had changed.

The Workers in the Vineyard

WHEN people came to see Jesus, and he was able to forgive them their sins, they had the chance to start again with a clean slate. One of Jesus's parables gave people a life-changing sense of freedom and hope. "There was once a land-owner who went out early one morning to the market place to hire workers," Jesus began. "He saw that there were many labourers waiting to be hired and he offered them the usual fee of one denarius per day. The men agreed and got down to work picking the grapes.

"Three hours later, the landowner went out again to the market place. Just as he had expected, several latecomers were hanging around hopefully.

"'If you're looking for work, go to my vineyard. I'll pay you a fair rate at the end of the day,' the landowner said.

"The pleased men hurried off straight away.

"At midday, the landowner went again to the market place and found workers who were delighted to be hired. And he went once more in the middle of the afternoon and picked up yet more grateful labourers.

"When there was only about one hour left before the

Treading grapes
In order to make wine, grapes need to be pressed to get the juice out. This was done by putting them into large vats and treading on them, as shown in this Byzantine mosaic from Beth-shan.

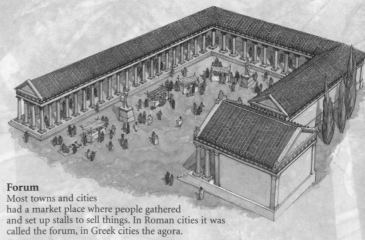

Forum
Most towns and cities had a market place where people gathered and set up stalls to sell things. In Roman cities it was called the forum, in Greek cities the agora.

labourers were due to down tools, the landowner hurried to the market place one last time, and soon there were even more workers in his vineyard. He didn't want them to feel unwanted and go home without any wages.

"As the sun set, the landowner told his steward to hand out the wages. The hot, exhausted men who had been working in the vineyard all day long were surprised when the landowner said, 'Pay the last shift of workers first.'

"'Evening shift – one denarius!' the steward announced, pressing a shiny coin into each of the worker's hands. The men were startled and delighted. A whole day's pay for less than an hour's work. How generous the landowner was!

"The mid-afternoon shift stepped forward. If those who have done less work than us have been paid one whole denarius, they wondered, how much will we be getting?

"'Mid-afternoon shift – one denarius!' the steward cried.

"At first, the labourers were disappointed. But they soon cheered up. We've still got a whole day's wages for less than a day's work, they thought.

"'Mid-day shift – one denarius!'

"This time the workers weren't at all pleased. Is this a joke? they wondered. We could have turned up at the very last minute and still have been paid the same!

> ❝ *Now when the first came, they thought they would receive more.* ❞

"And then the steward called out for a final time. 'Early-morning shift – one denarius!'

"There was nearly a riot. 'What do you mean by all this?' demanded the men. 'You've paid these shirkers the same as us, yet we've toiled in the scorching heat all day long!'

"The landowner was calm and kind. 'Friends,' he said. 'I'm not cheating you. Didn't we agree that you'd be paid one denarius? It's my choice to give these latecomers the same wages as you. Can't I spend my money as I like?'"

When Jesus explained the parable, his audience's hearts leapt. "The kingdom of heaven is like the landowner and his vineyard," Jesus said. "Even if you only find your way to God at the last minute, you'll still be as welcome as those who have been with God a long time."

Grape picking
Vineyards, places where people grow grape vines, were important in Israel. Vines grew well in the sunny climate, so grape production was an important part of the economy. They were eaten as fruit, and pressed to make wine. They were also dried to make cakes of raisins. This Egyptian wall painting shows grape pickers harvesting the crop.

❖ ABOUT THE STORY ❖

Jesus intended this parable to be applied in two ways. First, it applied to the newcomers to the faith who were despised by the "old guard". Secondly, it applied to those who would come to trust Jesus later from outside the Jewish religion. In heaven, He was saying, all are equal. This is not to encourage people to delay believing in Him, but to reassure those who realize at the last minute.

Blind Bartimaeus

EVERYBODY in Jericho knew Bartimaeus the beggar. He had been blind from birth and lived rough on the streets. Clutching his rags around him, he'd lift his dull eyes whenever he sensed people approaching and would hold out his begging bowl in hope. Occasionally, someone would take pity on him and drop a denarius into it. Bartimaeus was such a familiar figure that the people of Jericho had stopped thinking about his sad plight a long time ago.

One day used to seem very much like another for Bartimaeus. Every day he'd wake in darkness, sit by the roadside in darkness and then go to sleep in darkness.

But one morning, Bartimaeus got up to find that things were different. The road he sat beside was much busier than usual, and there were excited crowds hanging about all around him.

"What's going on?" Bartimaeus cried, as hoardes of people swept past him in both directions. "Who are you waiting for?"

"Jesus of Nazareth is going to pass by here on His way out of Jericho," said a voice.

Bartimaeus's pulse began to race. He had heard people talking about Jesus of Nazareth before. Bartimaeus thought that the man sounded amazing. People said that you had only to hear Him talk and your spirits would be lifted. They said that He healed lepers, cured paralytics and even raised dead people back to life! Bartimaeus had longed to encounter the preacher for himself. He was sure that if the great man could do all these wonderful things, He'd be able to make him see, too. But he had never dared to dream that he might actually get the chance to meet the holy man.

Now, hope suddenly flooded into the blind beggar.

"Son of David!" he began to shout, forgetting everyone around him in his desperation. "Have pity on me!"

From somewhere, Bartimaeus found a strength he never knew he had. He raised his voice louder, determined that Jesus should hear him. As he did so, the noise of the crowd grew more excited all around him, and Bartimaeus knew that the holy man was nearby.

"Jesus of Nazareth, please have mercy on me!" he yelled, his cries ringing out above the hubbub.

"Shut up, Bartimaeus!" came voices from all around.

❧ ABOUT THE STORY ❧

When Bartimaeus used the term "son of David" he was recognizing that Jesus was not just a remarkable man but that He was also the Messiah. It was this "faith" which Jesus commended. The blind man's prayer, too, was one of faith and dependence. He asked first and foremost for mercy. He knew that before God, everyone was a spiritual beggar, whether they were rich or poor.

Hebrew calendar
Bartimaeus didn't live by the calendar because every day was the same to him. This is a fragment of a Hebrew calendar. It is divided into twelve months, but they are different from ours.

Jesus healing
This old painting shows Jesus healing Bartimaeus. Healing was one way in which Jesus showed people God's love and compassion in action.

"We can't hear what he's saying."

But Bartimaeus just shouted louder than ever. "Jesus, son of David, take pity on me!"

"Bartimaeus, be quiet!" the voices came again – but this time they were filled with surprise. "Be quiet and listen! Jesus is calling for you. Quickly! Go to him."

In his hurry to get up, Bartimaeus got in a terrible tangle in his tattered cape. He ripped it from around him and threw it away, groping his way forwards. All of a sudden, he sensed Jesus was there, right in front of him. "Bartimaeus, what do you want from me?"

"Oh Lord," the beggar gasped, "please let me see." Bartimaeus felt gentle fingertips on his eyelids and immediately the gloom began to lift into a thick fog that swirled and cleared into a world of bright colours, the beauty of which he had never been able to imagine.

> He said, 'Lord, let me receive my sight.'

"Go in peace," Jesus said, "your faith has made you well." There was no way that the grateful beggar was going to leave the man who had given him such a precious gift. Joining on behind Jesus's disciples, Bartimaeus danced down the road, weeping aloud with joy and praising God.

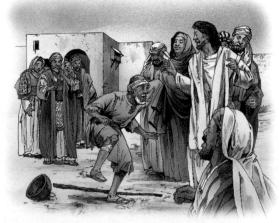

FAITH IS BELIEVING THAT GOD CAN DO WHATEVER HE WISHES, AND TRUSTING HIM TO DO WHAT WILL BRING HONOUR TO HIM AND BE BEST FOR US. FAITH LETS GOD DECIDE WHAT THOSE THINGS ARE.

Begging

Beggars were sadly a common sight in Bible times. They were often treated like vermin by some religious people, who believed that God had cursed them. Jesus went out of His way to help and heal poor people.

The Parable of the Wedding Feast

JESUS once said, "Many that are first will be last, and the last first." By this, He meant that some of the most important and distinguished people on earth will eventually be considered worthless by God; and many people who are looked down on and despised on earth will be precious in God's sight. If you were someone who always seemed to be down on your luck, Jesus's words were very comforting. If you fell into the "important and distinguished" category though, like the Pharisees, His words were deeply disturbing – not just a criticism, but a warning, too.

One night when Jesus had been invited to eat at the house of a Pharisee, Jesus told a story that He hoped would help His host to reach heaven.

"Once upon a time there lived a king who had a dearly beloved son. The prince was about to get married, and the king gave orders for a fantastic wedding banquet to be thrown. Only the very best would do for his son! Menus were discussed, recipes were tasted, wine was ordered, entertainment was booked, invitations were sent out, seating plans were drawn up, the silver was polished, flowers were arranged. And after months of preparation, all was finally ready. The delighted king sent out his servants to summon the guests to the celebrations.

"But they all returned alone. Trembling, they ventured before the king one by one and gave the guests' pathetic excuses. One guest said that he'd just bought a field and he really had to go out and plough it straight away. Another said that he'd just bought a herd of oxen to do some urgent work on his farm. A third said he couldn't come because he'd only just got married himself, and he couldn't leave his wife! And so it went on…

"The king was deeply offended and disappointed by the rudeness of his friends and relations.

"'Go and invite them again!' he roared, and sent the servants scurrying off once more.

"But yet again, not a single soul would come.

"'That's it! I've had enough of that ungrateful lot!' the king bellowed. 'They don't deserve to come and enjoy themselves here anyway.'

"He called for his servants one more time.

"'Go out into the streets and lanes of my kingdom,' he told them, 'and bring me all the homeless people you can find. The poor, the lame, the blind – invite them all! I'm going to give them the party of their lives! And give everyone a special robe to wear in honour of the occasion.'

"The banqueting hall was soon filled with the joyous sounds of feasting. And on the top table, the king was the happiest of all. He sat and watched the total strangers with the utmost pleasure. They seemed to be enjoying his hospitality far more than his friends and relations had ever done, and they were certainly more grateful.

"Suddenly, among the rows of guests with their richly decorated and brightly coloured clothes, the king's eyes fell on a man dressed in rags. His plate was piled high with food and he was tucking in, oblivious to everything and everyone around him. The king sprang angrily to his feet and marched down the rows of guests to where the man was seated.

"'Where is your robe?' the king demanded. 'Everyone invited by my servants was given a robe as a gift. Get out of here! You're an impostor!'

"While the man mumbled and spluttered, searching in vain for an excuse, the furious king called for his guards.

"'Tie him up and sling him outside into the darkness!' the king ordered. Then he gave the signal for the party to carry on…

> **For many are called, but few are chosen.**

"Remember," Jesus told the alarmed Pharisee who had invited Him to dinner, "many receive a special invitation to join God's kingdom, but only those who whole-heartedly want to be a part of it will be allowed to enter."

Wedding entertainment
Weddings in every culture often include singing and dancing. In Judea people sang and danced to the music of pipes and lyres. These are Egyptian musicians.

Hammurabi
Hammurabi was a king in Babylon about 1,800 years before Christ. He is pictured at the top left of this 2.5m (8 ft) obelisk, receiving laws from the god Shamash. Engraved on this obelisk are 280 laws relating to such things as marriage, as the King's son in this story, and murder. Some, but not all, of them are like the laws that God gave to Moses.

The Wise and Foolish Bridesmaids

IT was only natural that after listening to Jesus preach about the coming of the kingdom of heaven, people should ask, "Lord, when will this happen?"

Most of Jesus's disciples assumed that judgement day would be in the next few years, and certainly within their lifetimes. But Jesus explained to them in parables that only God knew when the end of the world would be.

"Picture ten bridesmaids at a wedding reception, waiting for the bride's new husband to arrive," Jesus told His disciples. "Darkness is falling, and the bridesmaids are standing outside with lamps to welcome the bridegroom in. But five of the bridesmaids have been foolish. They haven't thought to take flasks of spare oil with them.

"Unfortunately, there's no sign of the bridegroom. He's taking such a long time that the bridesmaids' legs begin to ache from standing up for so long, and they all sink to the floor for a short rest. One by one, their lamps grow short of oil and flicker out. In the quiet darkness, the weary bridesmaids all drift off to sleep.

"Suddenly they're being woken by a shout. 'The bridegroom is on his way! The bridegroom is on his way!'

"They spring to their feet. The wise bridesmaids refill their lamps with the oil they've brought and light them up. The foolish bridesmaids are left looking rather daft.

❖ ABOUT THE STORY ❖

Jesus said that when He returned to earth, the world as we know it would end. Evil would be punished, justice would be seen to be done and God's people would be united with Him for ever. Before that, He said, there would be many troubles that His people would need to be ready for. This story tells Christians to keep alert so they are ready for whatever God wants to them do.

A modern wedding
Marriage is a sign that a couple are leaving their old family and setting up a new family or household together. They pledge their faith to each other and also to God. This is a modern Jewish wedding, similar to the one Jesus's story is about.

IT WAS DIFFICULT FOR THE DISCIPLES TO UNDERSTAND THAT ONLY GOD KNEW WHEN JUDGEMENT DAY WOULD BE. JESUS SAID WE COULD BE JUDGED BY GOD AT ANY TIME, SO WE MUST ALWAYS BE READY. ∼

the five remaining bridesmaids hold their lamps high to light the way. Everyone bustles the laughing bridegroom into the house and when the last guest is inside, the door is closed behind them.

"When the five foolish bridesmaids return, their lamps lit once again, they are dismayed to find that they're locked out of the party. They bang on the door.

"'I'm sorry,' calls a voice, 'but I don't know you. I can't be sure who you are.'

"And the girls are left outside in the cold darkness.

"Don't be foolish like the five forgetful bridesmaids," Jesus warned His disciples urgently. "Make sure you're always prepared for God's coming, because you can never have any idea when it will be."

"'Please lend us some of your oil,' they ask their friends, somewhat sheepishly.

"The five sensible girls refuse. 'We're sorry, but we can't,' they explain. 'The bridegroom may still be a little way off yet, and if we share our oil with you, none of our lamps will last long enough. Why don't you hurry off and buy some more oil?'

> ❝ *And while they went to buy, the bridegroom came.* ❞

"The bridesmaids do as their more thoughtful friends suggest, and it just so happens that while they're gone, the bridegroom arrives. The guests all come out of the house to meet him, and amid much joyous singing and dancing,

Torchlight procession
At Jewish weddings in biblical times, the groom usually went to the bride's house, then took her to his house for the party, accompanied by an ever-growing procession of friends and relatives. Sometimes the party was held at the bride's house. Often the procession was at night, hence the need for the lamps, as there were no street lights.

Oil lamps
Oil lamps provided the main form of lighting in Bible times. The shallow bowl was filled with olive oil, and a wick was draped over the lip and lit. In the house they were placed on ledges.

The Parable of the Pounds

DESPITE all Jesus's teachings, as he drew nearer and nearer to Jerusalem some of His disciples became more and more convinced that the kingdom of God was about to appear. They still expected Jesus to lead a revolution in Jerusalem to overthrow the Romans. Jesus knew, as He'd already told His disciples, that far from gaining political power, He was going to be arrested, tried and eventually put to death.

"While you wait for the coming kingdom of the kingdom of God," Jesus said, "make the most of everything God has given you." Then Jesus told them this parable.

"A prince had to travel far away to claim a kingdom that was his rightful inheritance. As he would be away some time, he called his trusted servants to him.

"'Will you look after things for me while I am gone?' he asked them, and he gave them his bags of money for safe-keeping – five bags of gold to one servant, two bags to another servant and one bag of gold to a third servant. Then the prince left to claim his kingdom, leaving the men to decide what to do with their borrowed fortunes.

"Years passed, but the servants heard no word from their prince. Just as they began to wonder if they would ever see him again, he returned, now a king, with a kingdom and all the trappings that went with it. The celebrations went

on for weeks! Eventually he called his three trusted servants to him to ask them about his money.

"'Now, tell me what you did with my savings,' the king said, excitedly. 'Did you put them to good use?'

"The first servant hauled in ten sacks of coins.

"'Your highness,' he said. 'I decided to trade with your five bags of gold. I worked hard at it and I have made you another five bags on top.'

"The king was overjoyed. His servant had repaid his trust better than he could ever have imagined. 'Oh well done!' he cried. 'I shall reward you by making you governor over ten of my new cities.'

"Then the second servant came forward, heaving four bags of coins before the king. 'Your highness,' he said. 'I traded with your money, too, and have also doubled the sum. Here are four bags of gold.'

"The grateful king clapped his hands in delight. 'My thanks and congratulations to you, too!' he beamed. 'How would you like to be governor over five of my new cities?'

> ❝ *For to every one who has will more be given.* ❞

"Then the third servant stepped forwards, with only one, quite grubby, sack of money. He looked down at his feet and mumbled, 'Your highness, I didn't do anything with your money. I've seen how ruthless you can sometimes be and I was afraid. So I just hid the coins safely in the ground.' And the servant handed back the single bag of gold with which he had been entrusted.

"The king was hurt and annoyed. 'You mean to tell me that you have done nothing with my gift,' he boomed. 'How can you have been so idle? Even if you didn't feel able to trade with it yourself, you should have taken it to my bankers. They could have invested the money, so it was still being of some use.'

"The king swung round to his guards.

"'Take the money off this servant and give it to the man who made ten bags of money,' he commanded, 'then kick the worthless servant out. For those who are deserving and have worked hard for their reward will receive more. Those who haven't bothered to try, will have what little they possess taken away from them.'"

Banking

The Romans had a banking system, part of which was licensed by the state. The Jewish bankers tended to be moneylenders rather than savings bankers. This stone relief shows a Roman banker at his desk, perhaps in a market place.

Burying money

There were no banks for Jews to use at this time, no safe places to deposit metal ingots, coins or jewellery. People who wanted to hide their wealth buried it in the ground.

❖ **ABOUT THE STORY** ❖

This parable is often called "The parable of the talents" because the money or "pounds" were, in the original, "talents" which were units of weight for precious metals. And because we use the word "talent" to mean "what you are good at", it is an encouragement to use everything we have (not just money) to honour and serve God.

Important Teachings of Jesus

PEOPLE have always admired the teaching of Jesus in the Gospels. Some of His sayings have become part of everyday life: "Turn the other cheek"; "Go the second mile"; "Do to others as you would have them do to you". Jesus taught a lot of other things besides how to get on with our (sometimes difficult) neighbours. In fact, He mostly taught about God – what He is like and how we can get to know Him.

His key teaching was about the kingdom of God, which He said had arrived when He started His ministry. This wasn't a physical place; rather it was anywhere that God's rule was obeyed. He said it was growing from small beginnings like a big plant grows from a tiny seed, and that it grew alongside the kingdoms and values of this world like wheat growing among weeds. God's people – those who truly belonged to His kingdom – would be separated out from the rest on the day of judgement and spend eternity in heaven with God.

In order to enter the kingdom, people had to believe in Jesus. "Faith", to Jesus, was about trusting God. So He taught that God was like a loving parent who really did care for a child. Some people at the time thought God was a bit of an ogre. Not so, said Jesus in the Sermon on the Mount. If you know to give your child some bread to feed him when he's hungry, and not a stone to choke him, surely God will give us His loving gifts too.

Jesus taught His disciples to pray, asking God for all the things they needed and trusting Him to supply them. But He also warned them that they couldn't have everything they wanted. The Christian way, He said, was "a narrow way". It meant self-sacrifice – saying no to our desires in order to serve God and others first.

Part of that self-sacrifice was to be kind and loving to our neighbour, and in His parable of the good Samaritan, Jesus defined our neighbour as "anyone in need". He also said that a rich person should go and sell all his possessions and give the money to the poor. Jesus did not say that to every rich person, but in this case (as in others) the man's wealth was more important to him than God's kingdom. Jesus constantly challenged people to get their priorities right. Who was in charge of their life – them or God? What drove them – the desire to be rich and famous or the desire to honour God?

That was the point of the most famous collection of Jesus's teaching in what is known as the Sermon on the Mount. Some of it is repeated in the Sermon on the Plain in Luke 6, and both sermons are unlikely to have been taught at any one time. The Gospel authors have collected together some of Jesus's sayings into one place – He probably repeated them on many occasions.

The Sermon on the Mount begins with a reversal of normal human values and goes on to remind Christians that their role in the world is to be like salt, preserving it from going bad and being God's "flavour" or influence within it. Their "light" – their faith, applied in life – is to be seen, not hidden. Christianity, He is saying, is a public religion not a private philosophy.

In order to be salt and light in the world, Jesus's followers are to obey God completely and to aim for perfection, which is God's standard. People that are perfect in this way do not harbour anger against others, even if they have wronged them. They respect others, not treating them as objects who exist only to satisfy their desires.

Sermon on the Mount
The sermon that we are told in the gospel of Matthew that Jesus gave "on the mountain" has been described by some people as the first text on what it means to be a Christian and how one can lead a life following Jesus. It is as part of the Sermon on the Mount that Jesus teaches the people "The Lord's Prayer", and tells them that they can address God as the "heavenly Father".

Jesus and the apostles
Within His large group of followers Jesus chose a special few to whom He gave extra teaching. These men are normally called "apostles". The apostles were not always able to work out exactly what Jesus meant in His parables, so Jesus would explain to them what He meant.

Throughout the Bible, God is shown to keep His promises absolutely and to forgive sinners willingly. The person who follows Him is to be faithful and true as well, willing to help others and not to seek revenge or to stand in unfair judgement of others. They will then become generous to others, and their religious practice will be sincere, coming before all personal ambitions. Such an attitude is likely to experience real answers to prayer.

Jesus taught that if God really is in charge of your life, and you are seeking Him and His love above all else, then you'll discover the one thing everyone seeks: happiness. You won't have to worry, because you'll know that God is in charge and that He will provide all you need, even if He doesn't give you all you want.

You can also be assured that He'll help you at all times, even at the hardest times when you think you cannot carry on. Towards the end of His short life, Jesus told the disciples to expect to receive the power and help of God the Holy Spirit. He would help them to understand what Jesus had taught and would reassure them of God's loving presence at all times. He would also go ahead of them in their ministry, making people aware of their need for God.

In other words, being a follower of Jesus affected every part and every moment of a person's life. Jesus sometimes pictured the kingdom of God like buried treasure found in a field. The finder went and sold all he had in order to buy the field – and get the treasure. It was that valuable, and that important.

✦ THE BEATITUDES ✦

This well-known series of short sayings starts off Jesus's Sermon on the Mount. They are a guide for the people who wish to enter the kingdom of God. They start with the word "Blessed", which some versions of the Bible translate as "How happy". It means, "If you do what follows, you will receive God's kindness and blessing." Each is then followed by a promise. Probably the most famous of these is "Blessed are the meek, for they shall inherit the earth".

Beatitude	Means: If you are...	Then you will...
Poor in spirit	aware of your deep need of God	enter God's kingdom
Mourning	really sorry for your sins and the world's sin	know God's forgiveness and comfort
Meek, gentle	obedient to God in all ways	receive God's good gifts
Hungry for uprightness	longing to know God and do His will	be spiritually satisfied for ever
Merciful	sorry for others and helping them in their need	experience God's kindness
Pure in heart	sincere in every way	stay in touch with God
Peacemaker	helping enemies to become friends	be doing God's most important work
Persecuted	suffering for God's cause	be welcomed into heaven as a hero

Women in the Bible

THE Gospels deal with women in very different ways to how people would have expected at the time. The first announcement of the expected birth of Jesus, the promised Messiah, was to a woman (His mother) and after His birth, to shepherds. And the first appearance of Jesus after His resurrection was to women. Yet women and shepherds were regarded as inferior citizens. Their word was not trusted in a Jewish court. In a demonstration of the "good news of the kingdom", the Gospels show that Jesus came especially to show God's love to people who were despised by others.

During His lifetime, Jesus demonstrated that same concern and compassion. Although He did not break with His culture to the extent of having any women among His closest disciples, in all His dealings with them He treated women with dignity, respect and love. Indeed, without a large group of mostly anonymous women who provided food and shelter , the disciples would have had a much harder time. Some women, however, play a more prominent part in the Gospels.

Mary Magdalene

This Mary had a troubled past, but we are not told the details. Jesus had cast seven demons out of her, and she was devoted to Him with gratitude for the new life He had given her. She was at the cross when He died, and was the first to see Him alive three days later, although she at first thought He was the gardener.

Martha and Mary of Bethany

With their brother Lazarus, these two women were especially close to Jesus. They were probably unmarried (or possibly widowed) and invited Jesus to make their home a base when He was in the south of Judea.

One day Martha scurried around getting supper for Jesus and His disciples, annoyed that Mary, her (probably younger) sister, didn't help, but instead sat with the men listening to Jesus. Mary, Jesus said, had chosen the best option, taking advantage of a unique opportunity to learn about God. Her knowledge would remain for ever, but food could wait.

However, later at the tomb of Lazarus, Martha made a statement of faith in Jesus which is equal to that of Peter: "You are the Christ, the Son of the living God".

Salome

Salome is believed to have been the wife of Zebedee and mother of James and John, two of Jesus's closest disciples. She may also have been the sister of the Virgin Mary, and hence Jesus's aunt. She too was at the cross and witnessed the resurrection of Jesus.

TIMELINE

• Jesus performs the miracle of feeding five thousand people

AD30

JESUS FEEDING THE FIVE THOUSAND

LAVER BOWL

• Jesus walks over the Sea of Galilee towards the disciples' boat. Peter walks on water also, but loses his faith in Jesus and sinks

JESUS AND PETER

• Jesus calls Peter "the Rock" on which He will build His church

• The disciples Peter, James and John, witness Jesus transfigured into a heavenly being with Moses and Elijah

THE TRANSFIGURATION

Unnamed women Jesus helped

The "sinner" who anointed Jesus's feet while He ate supper in a Pharisee's house is not named in the Bible, but her devotion was commended and her faith brought her wholeness and healing.

So too did the woman caught in adultery (John 8:1–11). Here was an example of the double standards of the time. She was sentenced to death, but the man she had been with was not. Jesus simply said, "Whoever is without sin can cast the first stone", upholding the law but making it impossible for anyone to execute its sentence. Then, forgiving her, He said, "Go and sin no more." She had a new start.

The Virgin Mary, mother of Jesus

Pre-eminent among the saints, she conceived Jesus while a virgin as a unique sign that her child was the "Son of God" and also fully human at the same time. She was probably quite young at the time and was a woman of clear and trusting faith. During Jesus's childhood, when strange things happened (as when He remained for three days in the temple when He was twelve), Luke tells us that she "treasured these things in her heart" (Luke 2:51).

She was present at the cross, grieving at His death, and Jesus showed His great love and compassion for her by asking John to take Mary and look after her. She was also one of the first witnesses of His resurrection. However, she is not mentioned in the rest of the New Testament.

☙ WORSHIPPING MARY ❧

Later in church history Mary was declared to have been taken bodily into heaven (without dying). Many people pray to her today as one of the saints.

Shrine
This is a traditional shrine to Mary that has been built at the side of the road.

JESUS AND THE SINNING WOMAN

• Pharisees send soldiers to arrest Jesus, but they return without Him

• Jesus teaches the people about the power of prayer

• Jesus tells the stories of the prodigal son and the good samaritan

• Jesus cures ten lepers, but only one Samaritan man comes to thank Him

JESUS AND THE LEPERS

• Jesus forgives the corrupt tax collector Zacchaeus in the city of Jericho

JESUS AND MARY

LAZARUS RAISED FROM THE DEAD

• Jesus visits His friends Mary and Martha in Bethany and raises Lazarus from the dead

AD33

Glossary

apostle
The group of twelve men that Jesus picked from His disciples were called apostles. They were the closest people to Him, and learned the most from Him. The group of apostles also includes Saul, who converted to Christianity after Jesus's death.

baptism
Jesus commanded that His followers be baptised to show they had been converted. Baptism involves immersing people in water. The Jews used to baptize people into the faith as a sign of cleansing. John the Baptist baptized many people as a sign of repentance and inner cleansing, but the apostle Paul later said that Christian baptism is symbolic; when the person disappears beneath the water and then reappears, the are symbolically undergoing death, burial and resurrection, as Christ did.

communion
A ceremony that takes place in church, where Christians eat bread and drink wine in remembrance of the body and blood of Christ, who died on the cross.

disciples
As Jesus travelled round Galilee, teaching and preaching to the people there, people started to follow Him and His way of living. These people were called disciples. From the larger group of the disciples, Jesus chose his particularly close group of followers, called the apostles.

Gentile
This is a general terms for 'nations', and which came to mean 'anyone who is not Jewish'. Jesus made sure that he preached His message to Gentiles as well as Jews.

kingdom of God
The kingdom of God is not an earthly kingdom. Jesus said that the kingdom of God is within everyone who follows His teachings, and tries to live in a Christian way.

Levite
Members of the tribe of Levi, they were chosen to serve God, firstly in the Tabernacle, during the time of Moses, and then in the temple.

messiah
This means 'anointed one' in Hebrew, the word "Christ" is the equivalent word in Greek. It means one chosen by God. By the time of Jesus all the Jews were hoping for a great Messiah-king to set up an everlasting kingdom. Jesus's kingdom, the kingdom of God, was not an earthly kingdom, and Jesus was not an emperor commanding armies as may were expecting. But the kingdom of God will last forever.

miracle
Jesus performed many miracles during his ministry in Galilee, healing the sick and dying, casting out demons, and even bringing people back from the dead. Miracles are sometimes described as "mighty works", and they are performed through the power of God. The greatest and most important miracle is the resurrection of Jesus.

parable
Jesus told stories to people, called parables, to teach them about the kingdom of God. The stories used people and situations that his audience would have been familiar with, which made the point of Jesus's story easier to remember.

Pharisee
A strict religious sect, the name Pharisee means "separated ones". They were generally ordinary people, not priests, who closely followed Jewish law. Sometimes they extended the ways that these laws were applied to make them even harder to follow. For example, when they said that people must not work on the Sabbath, they meant people could not walk more than about 1km from their house, or even light a fire in their house.

repentance
If a person repents, it means that they are truly sorry for their sins. Jesus forgave the sins of those people who came to Him and were genuinely sorry for what they had done. But it also means being determined to leave sin behind, trying not to sin at all in future.

resurrection
Three days after Jesus died on the cross, He came back to life, He was resurrected. This is the main and central point of the New Testament, and of Christianity. Jesus's resurrection was witnessed by the disciples, whom Jesus visited in the time before he ascended to heaven.

Sadducees
These were a group of people smaller than the Pharisees, but more influential. Most of them were members of the family of priests. Most of the information that we have comes from their enemies so is not very reliable. We do know that they did not agree with the extensions of the law that the Pharisees tried to impose on people. This is why the Sadducees did not believe in life after death, as this is not mentioned in the Old Testament.

Samaritan
When the Promised Land was conquered by the Babylonian Empire and the Jews were taken away to live in Babylon, a period known as the Exile, the city of Samaria was filled with people from other lands, taken there by the Babylonians. These people were hated by the Jews after this time for taking the Jews' cities. Jesus makes sure that He demonstrates his concern for them, and shows that the kingdom of God is open to everyone by using the Samaritans in his stories, most famously in the story of the good Samaritan.

Index

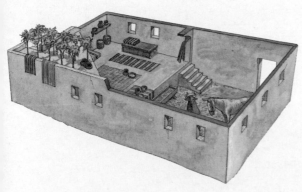